Collectible German Animals Value Guide

1948 - 1968

An Identification and Price Guide to Steiff, Schuco, Hermann and Other German Companies

by Dee Hockenberry

Photographs
by Tom Hockenberry

Steiff Musical Teddy Bear $900; Steiff City Mouse $125; Schuco Teddy Bear $800

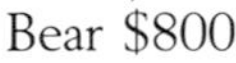

Hobby House Press ™

Acknowledgements

A special word of thanks to the following people:

To Lorraine Oakley for her unfailing support and always finding time in her busy schedule to type for me.

To Donna H. Felger, my editor.

To Gary R. Ruddell for thinking it was a good idea in the first place.

To my collector friends who were so willing to share their treasures with me.

To the many people I have met through my association with soft toys who encouraged me to write this book.

And finally to my husband, Tom, always there, always willing to devote hours on the animal kingdom.

My love and gratitude to you all.

Extra Photo Credits

Ruth Baum Collection: Herself, Elaine Bosler Collection: Michelle Daunton, Barbara Chadwick Collection: Dennis Yusa, Mary Phillips Collection: Michelle Daunton, Michelle Daunton Collection: Herself, Deborah Pugliani Collection: Louis Pugliani, Kay Skogland Collection: Herself, Dennis Yusa Collection: Himself.

The values given within this book are intended as value guides rather than arbitrarily set prices. The values quoted are as accurate as possible but in the case of errors, typographical, clerical or otherwise, the author and publisher assume no liability nor responsibility for any loss incurred by users of this book.

Additional copies of this book may be purchased at $9.95
from
Hobby House Press, Inc.
Cumberland, Maryland 21502
or from your favorite bookstore or dealer.
Please add $1.75 for postage.

Printed in the United States of America

ISBN: 0-87588-337-0

Table of Contents

Schuco Yes/no Teddy Bear.
$700-up. See page 107.

Foreword

I have categorized and documented the Teddy Bears and animals in this book to the best of my ability. As in all collectibles, there are variables and this should be taken into consideration.

My method of grading is as follows: Tissue mint designates store new condition with all tags, labels and buttons intact. Otherwise, the rating refers to the condition of the piece itself, regardless of the absence or presence of identifying marks. Steiff ribbons *usually* have a woven edge. Teddy Bears (except for dressed and "Teddy Baby") normally came from the factory decorated in this manner. The bows on bears are the ones most frequently removed at some point. Schuco bears, because of the bow attached "Tricky" tag, did not have neck adornments. In most instances, the ribbons, etc., have been added for decorative purposes.

The prices are meant to be a guide and not taken as absolute. Prices given are for the animal pictured, taking into account the size, condition, identification marks and rarity. Prices vary from area to area as well as abroad. Availability plays a role — the rarer commanding a higher value. Auction prices may greatly exceed those given and should be acknowledged as what the buyer is willing to pay and not necessarily its true worth. If you find a toy priced a great deal lower, you probably have found a bargain. Finally, pay what you comfortably can. You may never find it again.

Why Do Adults Collect Toys?

When the genesis for this book was taking form and discussed with the publisher, Gary R. Ruddell, one of the questions pondered upon was why adults collect toys. One hypothesis suggested by Mr. Ruddell was related to the issue of the *Shirley Temple* doll. He recalled a woman telling him that as a child her parents could not afford to give her one. As a young woman she was willing to pay the vast increase such a collectible demands and at last realized her dreams.

This conversation caused me to reflect as well. I suspect that statistics would reveal more cash outlay on toys for grown-ups than for children. As a child raised during the Depression, I certainly was not inundated with gifts. I did have a *Shirley Temple* doll, however, given to me while in the hospital for a tonsillectomy. I recall other toys as well and do not remember a feeling of deprivation. So why do I collect? I do not know for sure but it may be the thrill of the chase as much as anything. In the interest of solvency, I try in my own collecting fever to stay within the bounds of certain areas. I love many more than I actually amass but fortunately, as a dealer, I am able to enjoy many, if only for a brief time, before they find a permanent home.

I have talked to people who are seeking a toy they had as a child and so I believe that nostalgia certainly plays a very large part. Of course, in this pursuit people come across other wonderful toys and a collector is born. Still the cry "Teddy come home!" remains a driving force.

The average collector finds a fascination for nearly all toys of a bygone era. They seem to possess a charm not found in the toys of today. The attention to detail, the patina of age and certainly the durability of even seemingly fragile items causes a sense of wonder.

The market for Steiff items from the 1950s is perhaps the broadest. It is the decade when Steiff, as well as other companies, reached a zenith in exportation. Steiff, in fact, made many products solely for the United States. Many, many young people collect Steiff from this era because they were given to them as children. Their toys are in remarkable condition, attesting to the fact that even as tots they recognized their uniqueness and treated them with respect. They continue adding to the collection, amassing hundreds of soft toys. Thus, it can be said that although they themselves are only in their mid thirties, they have been collectors for thirty years. I call that advanced. This group appears to be the most avid in their pursuit.

Many of the toys in this book have been personally handled by me during the course of business. Others are pictured through the generosity of friends and fellow collectors. The common threads that bind us together is our willingness to share our finds with others.

It is amazing to contemplate how much more is known and documented since the first books on soft toys were published. It is this sharing among us that enables us to learn and grow. I thank with all my heart those who taught me and hope this book answers some questions as well.

Finally, whether it be nostalgia for days-gone-by or just an innate love for precious things, collecting Teddy Bears and animals appears to be here to stay. Whatever the reason, I think we all agree it is a wondrous feeling to leave cares and worries behind and just be a kid again.

Steiff Teddy Bears and Animals

The 1950s are often referred to as Steiff's heyday for exportation. Toy production was in full swing and they found in the United States a market eager for their quality and varied examples. It is animals from this decade that the majority of collectors seek today. It is a tribute to see how well preserved they are and how many can be located with the button and chest tag still intact.

Domestic and wild animals of every breed and description appear to have been made and the attention to detail makes them instantly recognizable. Cats and dogs are extremely popular and the shorter the production, the more eagerly sought. The black Scotty dog, the white Sealyham and the St. Bernard (especially the one with the whiskey cask) are among the breeds hardest to locate. "Laika," the Russian space dog is another elusive creature. The larger size is especially beautiful with the paperweight eyes a focal point.

"Tapsy," the brown and white tabby and "Gussy," the long-haired black and white cat are among the two felines who prove to be the more rare.

Because the toys were made for children, it is easy to understand why some, such as the bat and spider, were not widely popular. Production was limited and it is this reason why the pursuit of them is so nearly frenzied today.

There are other animals perhaps even rarer, but so little is known of them that the demand is not as great. It is the wise collector who recognizes this and quietly invests when such a find crosses his path.

Although there are collectors who "Think Big" and the largest size is the most difficult to locate, it has been my experience to find the smallest size most in demand. The delicate perfection or the fact that so many more can be stored may be the reason. The choice is so wide and varied that even the most advanced collectors are still pursuing Steiff with unabated enthusiasm.

Steiff Identification Marks

Toy production accelerated following World War II. Germany was divided and from about 1948 to 1953 some manufacturers identified their toys according to area. The Steiff company used a cloth tag sewn into a seam and labeled "U S Zone-Germany." Very often only a fragment of this tag remains but regardless of legibility, collectors are delighted to have items with this form of identification.

Absolute dating is difficult but in general there are some guidelines to follow. For a short span in the 1940s, the ear button appeared with "STEIFF" block printed and raised, but lacking the trailing final "F" as on earlier items. Not many of these buttons surface.

During the 1950s and into the early 1960s, the button remained with the letters raised but in script. In this book when referring to raised buttons, it always means script method unless otherwise noted. Attachment was by a two-prong method. The yellow stock tag in back of the button reveals numbers divided by a slash. On dolls the button and stock tag is usually attached to a plastic wrist bracelet rather than in the ear.

In the late 1960s the button changed to incised lettering (still script) and a comma replaced the slash on the stock tag. Attachment changed to a rivet so if the button is not present, a hole remains in the ear rather than two tiny slashes left behind as would be found by prongs.

Summarily, as regards to my identification of the animals labeled marks, the era of a raised button is most often the 1950s and early 1960s.

The chest tag remained the same during the years that this book deals with. Made of paper, it is round and has a smiling bear's head at the bottom. Tags may have the name of the animal as given by the company; for instance, the goat named "Zicky." In some cases the generic name is used as in the "Skunk," or, and this is usually of the 1960 era, "Original Steiff."

Wooden toys display a small brass placque with the Steiff name and logo embossed.

Some variables exist that could cause confusion. Very often an older button and tag were used at the factory (perhaps if they ran out?) on newer stock. It is my understanding, as well, that if an item is sent to the factory for repair and lacks identification, a new form is applied. This surely identifies it as Steiff, but adds to the mystery.

In the final anaylsis, the best defense is to arm yourself with as much knowledge as possible by handling and studying the toys.

Steiff Teddy Bear: 19½in (50cm)
Caramel mohair; brown glass eyes; felt pads; excelsior stuffed; all jointed; tissue mint; reasonably easy to find.
MARKS: Raised button; chest tag
PRICE: $700-up

Steiff Teddy Bear: 8in (20cm)
Gold mohair; brown glass eyes; felt pads; excelsior stuffed; all jointed; tissue mint; reasonably easy to find.
MARKS: Raised button; chest tag
PRICE: $300

Barbara Chadwick and Dennis Yusa Collection.

Steiff Teddy Bear: 11in (28cm)

Caramel mohair; felt pads; glass eyes; excelsior stuffed; all jointed; slight mohair wear; somewhat easy to find. Circa 1955.

MARKS: Signed on foot by Hans Otto Steiff

PRICE: $275

Steiff Teddy Bear: 11in (28cm)

Tan mohair; felt pads; glass eyes; excelsior stuffed; all jointed; near mint; somewhat hard to find with this ID.

MARKS: Raised button; U S Zone tag

PRICE: $350

Steiff Teddy Bears:

Gold mohair; felt pads; brown glass eyes; excelsior stuffed; all jointed; mint, largest harder to find.

30in (76cm) described elsewhere

28in (71cm)
MARKS: U S Zone tag
PRICE: $2200

14in (36cm)
MARKS: Raised button; chest tag
PRICE: $400

11in (28cm)
MARKS: Chest tag
PRICE: $325

9in (23cm). Circa 1950.
MARKS: No ID
PRICE: $275

Michelle Daunton Collection.

Steiff Teddy Bear: 30in (76cm)

Gold mohair; felt pads; brown glass eyes; excelsior stuffed; all jointed; mint; rare size.

MARKS: U S Zone tag

PRICE: $2500

Michelle Daunton Collection.

Steiff Teddy Bear: 30in (76cm)

Long tan curly mohair; felt pads with bottom cardboard lined; brown glass eyes; excelsior stuffed; all jointed; toy horn not original; mint; rare size.

MARKS: U S Zone tag

PRICE: $2400

Michelle Daunton Collection.

Steiff Teddy Bears: 3½in (9cm)

Left: Beige mohair; all jointed; black bead eyes; excelsior stuffed; mint; reasonably easy to find.
MARKS: Raised button
PRICE: $200-up

Right: Beige mohair; swivel head; black bead eyes; soft stuffed; mint; reasonably easy to find.
MARKS: Incised button
PRICE: $40-up

Steiff Teddy Bear: 3½in (9cm)

Gold mohair; no pads; black glass eyes; excelsior stuffed; all jointed; excellent condition; rare to find with all ID.
MARKS: Raised button; chest tag; remnant U S Zone tag
PRICE: $275-up

Steiff Teddy Bears: 5½in (14cm)

Left: Gold mohair; all jointed; brown glass eyes; excelsior stuffed; no pads; mint; harder to find than larger sizes.
MARKS: Raised button
PRICE: $200

Right: Brown mohair; all jointed; brown glass eyes; excelsior stuffed; no pads; lace collar not original; excellent condition; brown rarer than gold. Circa 1955.
MARKS: No ID
PRICE: $250

Steiff Teddy Bear: 17in (43cm)

Tan mohair; all jointed; brown glass eyes; excelsior stuffed; felt pads; near mint; rare with this ID.
MARKS: Block printed button; U S Zone tag
PRICE: $700

Steiff Teddy Bear: 13-1/2in (34cm)
Gold mohair; all jointed; brown glass eyes; excelsior stuffed; felt pads; near mint; reasonably easy to find.
MARKS: Raised button
PRICE: $350-up

Steiff Teddy Bear: 15in (38cm)
Off-white mohair; brown glass eyes; excelsior stuffed; felt pads; all jointed; mint; white color hard to find.
MARKS: Raised button
PRICE: $600-up
Lorraine Oakley Collection.

Steiff Teddy Bear: 12in (31cm)

Caramel mohair; sheared inset snout extending around eyes; plastic eyes; velour pads; excelsior stuffed; all jointed; excellent condition; easy to find.

MARKS: Incised button

PRICE: $95

Carol Alabiso Collection.

Steiff "Teddy-Baby": 3-1/2in (10cm)

Gold mohair; brown glass eyes; closed mouth; sheared feet; all jointed; near mint; very rare size.

MARKS: Chest tag; U S Zone tag

PRICE: $900-up

Dennis Yusa Collection

Steiff "Teddy Baby": 15-3/4in (40cm)
Blonde mohair with sheared snout and top of feet; tan leatherette pads; open felt mouth; brown glass eyes; excelsior stuffed; all jointed; missing collar and bell, necklace not original; mint; hard-to-find size.
MARKS: Raised button
PRICE: $1400
Ruth Baum Collection.

Steiff "Teddy-Baby": 15-3/4in (40cm)
Brown mohair; sheared tan mohair snout and tops of feet; tan felt open mouth and pads; brown glass eyes; excelsior stuffed; all jointed; collar and bell; mint; hard-to-find size.
MARKS: Raised button
PRICE: $1500
Ruth Baum Collection.

LEFT: Steiff Zotty Teddy Bears:

19in (48cm)
MARKS: Raised button
PRICE: $595-up
14in (36cm)
MARKS: Raised button; chest tag
PRICE: $400
8in (20cm). Circa 1955.
MARKS: No ID
PRICE: $250
Sleeping 7½in (19cm)
MARKS: Incised button
PRICE: $95

Tan frosted mohair; felt pads; open felt-lined mouth; brown glass eyes; excelsior stuffed; all jointed; growler in largest; near mint; reasonably easy to find; applies to all except sleeping who is soft stuffed; non jointed; airbrushed toes on rear pads; embroidered sleep eyes.

Barbara Chadwich and Dennis Yusa Collection.

RIGHT: Steiff Teddy Bears, "Jackie" and "Teddy-Baby":

Left: "Jackie": 9-1/2in (24cm)
Blonde mohair; all jointed; brown glass eyes; excelsior stuffed; felt pads; pink stitch on nose; airbrushed belly button; came with booklet; excellent condition; rare.
MARKS: Raised button
PRICE: $1200

Right: "Teddy Baby": 11in (28cm)
Blonde mohair with sheared mohair muzzle and feet; all jointed; brown glass eyes; leatherette pads; cardboard-lined feet to facilitate standing; open felt-lined mouth; downward curve to paws; 3 other sizes; also brown mohair; excellent condition; bell missing from collar; hard to find.
MARKS: Raised button; U S Zone tag
PRICE: $850 *Barbara Chadwick and Dennis Yusa Collection.*

Steiff "Zotty" Teddy Bear: 20in (51cm)
Pinky tan curly mohair, sheared muzzle; open felt-lined mouth; felt pads; soft and hard stuffed; brown glass eyes; mint; reasonably easy to find. Circa 1950.
MARKS: No ID (Signed on foot by H.O.S.)
PRICE: $500-up
Lorraine Oakley Collection.

Steiff "Zotty" Teddy Bear: 30in (76cm)

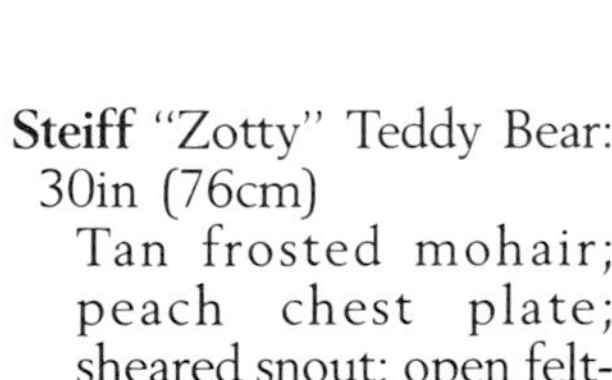

Tan frosted mohair; peach chest plate; sheared snout; open felt-lined mouth; felt pads; bottom pads lined with cardboard; brown glass eyes; excelsior stuffed; all jointed; mint; hard-to-find size. Circa 1950.
MARKS: No ID
PRICE: $850-up
Elaine Bosler Collection.

Steiff "Orsi" Teddy Bear: 10in (25cm)
Brown mohair; sheared tan mohair snout; open felt mouth; brown glass eyes; felt pads; hard and soft stuffed; swivel head and arms; red felt bib; mint; hard to find.
MARKS: Raised button
PRICE: $495

Steiff "Baren Marke" Teddy Bear: 13¾in (35cm)
Caramel woolly plush; sheared tan mohair snout; open red felt mouth with tongue; black glass eyes; felt pads; soft and hard stuffed; fully jointed; produced for "Baren Marke" coffee cream; shown with this company's product. German market only; rare.
MARKS: Raised button
PRICE: $800-up
Ruth Baum Collection.

TOP: **Steiff** Teddy Bear: 7in (18cm)
Tan mohair; lighter tan on chest; limbs jointed; brown glass eyes; no paw pads; felt pads on feet; excelsior stuffed; tail moves head in a nearly circular movement; excellent condition; rare. Circa 1955.
MARKS: No ID
PRICE: $800

BOTTOM: **Steiff** "Breuni" Teddy Bear: 5⅛in (13cm)
Gold mohair head and legs; glass eyes; excelsior stuffed; swivel head; felt gloves and foot pads; cotton clothes; mint; rare.
MARKS: Raised button; chest tag
PRICE: $400

Steiff "Musical" Teddy Bear: 13in (33cm)
Described fully elsewhere; this one near mint with original felt circle.
MARKS: Raised button
PRICE: $1400

Steiff "Baggy" Teddy Bear: 8¾in (22cm)
Soft white wool made like the wool ball birds; mohair ears; plastic eyes. This bear has an old button with the printed "f" underscored, an indication that an older button was used on a postwar product. A good example of how confusing absolute dating can be. Rare.
MARKS: Printed button; hand lettered ear tag.
PRICE: $350-up

Ruth Baum Collection.

Steiff "Musical" Teddy Bear: 13½in (34cm)

Tan mohair; felt pads; brown glass eyes; excelsior stuffed; all jointed; bellows music box; felt circle replaced — originally had music in gold lettering; some fur loss on head; rare. Circa 1950.

MARKS: No ID

PRICE: $900

Steiff "Lully" Teddy Bear: 8½in (22cm)

Tan, white and gold mohair; open felt mouth; swivel head; excelsior stuffed; brown glass eyes; mint; somewhat hard to find.

MARKS: Raised button; chest tag

PRICE: $130

Deborah Pugliani Collection.

Steiff Teddy Bear Hockey Player: 11in (28cm)

Tan dralon; all jointed; brown plastic eyes; soft stuffed; felt pads; open mouth; blue dralon forms clothes; red jersey-like pants; paper number; near mint; hard to find with skates.

MARKS: Incised button; chest tag

PRICE: $350

Steiff "Petsy" Teddy Bear: 11in (28cm)

Tan plush; felt pads; plastic eyes; soft stuffed; tissue mint; hard to find in this condition and with all ID.

MARKS: Incised button; chest tag; dralon tag

PRICE: $125-up

Steiff "Cosy" Teddy Bear: 11in (28cm)

White plush; brown chest plate; plastic eyes; soft stuffed; open mouth; felt pads; hard to find in this condition and with all ID.

MARKS: Incised button; chest tag; dralon tag

PRICE: $125-up

Steiff Teddy Bear Hand Puppet: 9in (23cm)

Brown mohair; sheared tan snout; brown glass eyes; open felt mouth; tissue mint; somewhat easy to find.

MARKS: Raised button; chest tag

PRICE: $75

Barbara Chadwick Collection.

Steiff Bear on Fours: 9in (23cm)
Brown mohair; tan sheared snout; brown glass eyes; felt pads; near mint; somewhat hard to find.
MARKS: U S Zone tag
PRICE: $175

Teddy Bear: 3½in (9cm)
Tan mohair; brown glass eyes; no pads; excelsior stuffed; all jointed; near mint; somewhat hard to find. Circa 1955.
MARKS: No ID
PRICE: $200-up

Teddy Bear: 3½in (9cm)
Gold mohair; same description as other one; tissue mint; hard to find.
MARKS: Raised button; chest tag
PRICE: $275

Dennis Yusa Collection.

Steiff Panda: 11in (30cm)
Steiff made this size panda in the 1950s; however, this one is likely circa 1930. Description would be the same except older has felt pads; later one more usual to have suedene.
PRICE: 1950s Era-$800-up

Steiff Panda: 8in (20cm)
Black and white mohair; brown glass eyes; open felt mouth; suedene pads; all jointed; sheared mohair top of feet; excellent condition; hard to find.
MARKS: Raised button
PRICE: $650-up

Steiff Panda: 6in (15cm)
Description same as above.
MARKS: Raised button
PRICE: $350

Lorraine Oakley Collection.

Steiff Panda: 20in (51cm)
Black and white mohair; suedene pads (felt cardboard lined;) brown glass eyes; open felt mouth; excelsior stuffed; near mint; hard to find. Circa 1955.
MARKS: Signed on foot "H.O. Steiff"
PRICE: $1250

Lorraine Oakley Collection.

Steiff Polar Bear: 6in (15cm)
White mohair; sheared muzzle; blue glass eyes; excelsior stuffed; felt pads; collar with bell; mint; the larger 9in (23cm) size harder to find.
MARKS: Raised button
PRICE: $150

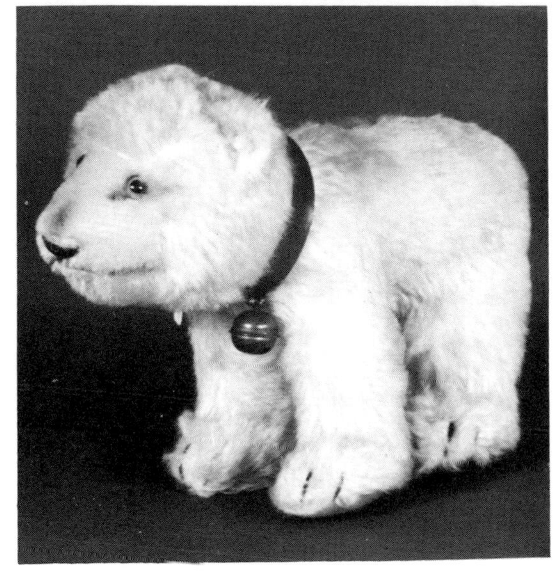

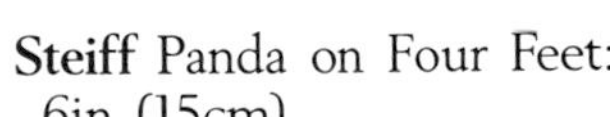

Steiff Panda on Four Feet: 6in (15cm)
Black and white mohair; felt pads; glass eyes; swivel head; leather collar; near mint; somewhat hard to find.
MARKS: Raised button
PRICE: $140
Lorraine Oakley Collection.

Steiff "Tapsy" Cat: 4in (10cm)

White and brown striped mohair; green glass eyes; excelsior stuffed; came in three other sizes; excellent condition; hard to find.

MARKS: Chest tag

PRICE: $95

Steiff "Snurry" Cats: 4½in (12cm) and 6in (15cm)

Tan and brown striped mohair; excelsior stuffed; embroidered sleep eyes; excellent condition; hard to find.

MARKS: Raised buttons

PRICE: 4½in (12cm) $140

6in (15cm) $155

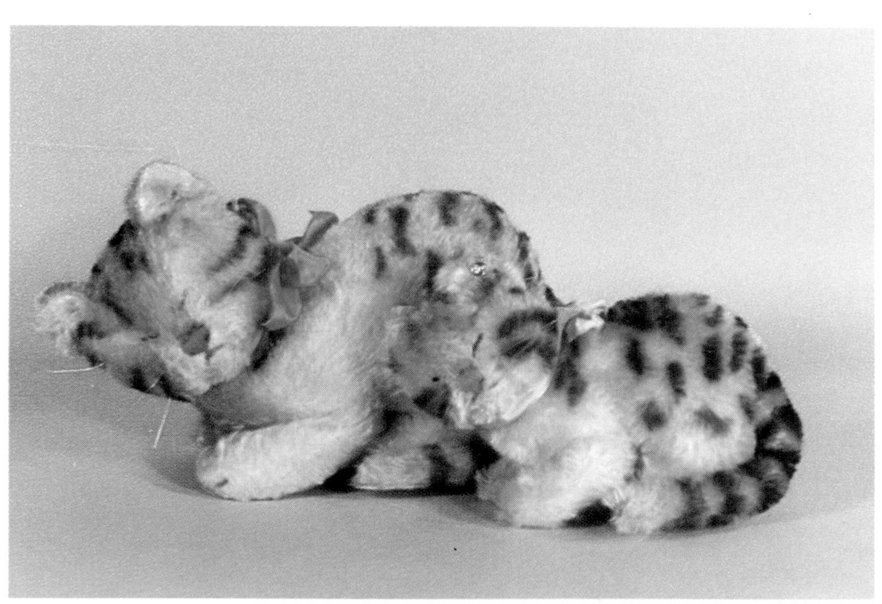

Steiff "Gussy" Cat: 4in (10cm)
Black and white mohair; green glass eyes; hard stuffed; swivel head; excellent condition; somewhat rare.
MARKS: Raised button; chest tag
PRICE: $100-up

Steiff "Sulla" Cat: 6½in (17cm)
Gray dralon with tan mohair bib; soft stuffed; green glass eyes; airbrushed toes; excellent condition; rare.
MARKS: Raised button
PRICE: $60

Steiff "Lizzy" Cat: 6½in (17cm)

White and gray striped mohair; green glass eyes; excelsior stuffed; upright tail; excellent condition, reasonably easy to find.

MARKS: Incised button

PRICE: $80

Steiff "Fiffy" Cat: 7in (18cm)

Off-white and gray striped mohair; green glass eyes; excelsior stuffed; near mint; hard to find.

MARKS: Raised button

PRICE: $150

Steiff Siamese Cat: 3½in (9cm)

Tan shaded mohair; open felt mouth; brilliant blue glass eyes; excelsior stuffed; mint; rare. Circa 1953.

MARKS: No ID

PRICE: $125

Deborah Pugliani Collection.

Steiff Siamese Kitten: 6in (15cm)

Tan and brown mohair; excelsior stuffed; blue glass eyes; felt-lined ears; bell attached to chest; excellent condition; rare.

MARKS: Raised button

PRICE: $140

Steiff "Diva" Cat: 13¾in (35cm)

Long white dralon; large yellow glass eyes; soft and hard stuffed; mint; hard to find.

MARKS: Incised button; chest tag.

PRICE: $140-up

Deborah Pugliani Collection.

Steiff "Kitty-Cat": 8in (20cm) by 10in (25cm)
Gray-white and dark gray striped mohair; all jointed; excelsior stuffed; green glass eyes; excellent condition; rare this size and darker stripes.
MARKS: Raised button
PRICE: $150

Steiff "Tabby" Cat on Eccentric Wheels: 6½in (17cm)
White and gray striped mohair; green glass eyes; hard to find; wear on wheels/otherwise excellent.
MARKS: Raised button
PRICE: $175

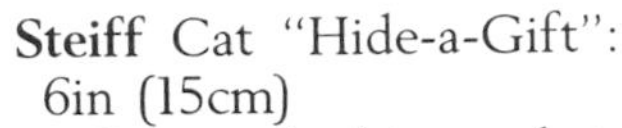

Steiff Cat "Hide-a-Gift": 6in (15cm)

Gray and white mohair head and arms; green glass eyes; felt dress; meant to hide small gifts under skirt; mint; somewhat easy to find; other animals produced as well.

MARKS: Chest tag

PRICE: $55-up

Steiff "Kalac" Cat: 14in (36cm)

Black and white mohair; all jointed; excelsior and soft stuffed; gold plastic eyes; tissue mint; very rare.

MARKS: Incised button; chest tag

PRICE: $650-up

Steiff "Sulac" Cocker: 15¾in (40cm)
Mohair in shades of gold; black and white eyes; soft and hard stuffed; all jointed with dangling legs; mint; rare. The cat described elsewhere.
MARKS: Raised button; chest tag
PRICE: $650-up
Ruth Baum Collection.

Steiff Basset Hound: 5in (13cm)
Tan and white mohair; black and white plastic eyes; excelsior stuffed; excellent condition; somewhat easy to find.
MARKS: Raised button
PRICE: $95

Steiff Collie: 15in (38cm)
Vari-colored long and short mohair; brown glass eyes; open mouth with tongue; excelsior stuffed; near mint; hard to find in this large size.
MARKS: Raised button; chest tag
PRICE: $125

Steiff Boxer: 4in (10cm)
Dark apricot shaded mohair; black velvet muzzle; glass eyes; excelsior stuffed; collar; reasonably easy to find; tissue mint.
MARKS: Incised button; chest tag
PRICE: $75

Steiff "Laika" Russian Space Dog: 9in (24cm)
White and tan airbrushed mohair; excelsior stuffed; paperweight-style brown and white glass eyes; collar; also made in 6in (15cm) size; rare; tissue mint.
MARKS: Raised button; chest tag
PRICE: $625

Note: The poodle, "Snobby", is very common and unlike these rare examples. Do not confuse.
Ruth Baum Collection.

Steiff "Tosi" Poodle: 8⅝in (22cm)
White plush; brown glass eyes; excelsior stuffed; mint; rare.
MARKS: Raised button; U S Zone tag
PRICE: $200

Steiff "Tosi" Poodle: 5½in (14cm)
Black plush; brown glass eyes; excelsior stuffed; collar; mint; rare.
MARKS: Raised button; U S Zone tag
PRICE: $150

Steiff "Walther" Poodle: 11⅞in (30cm)
Gray long and short mohair; applied painted leather-like eyes and nose; excelsior stuffed; mint; rare.
MARKS: Raised button
PRICE: $450

Steiff "Arco" German Shepherd: 7in (18cm)
White, brown and black mohair; excelsior stuffed; brown glass eyes; open mouth with tongue; missing collar; ribbon and ball not original; excellent condition; reasonably easy to find.
MARKS: Raised button
PRICE: $105

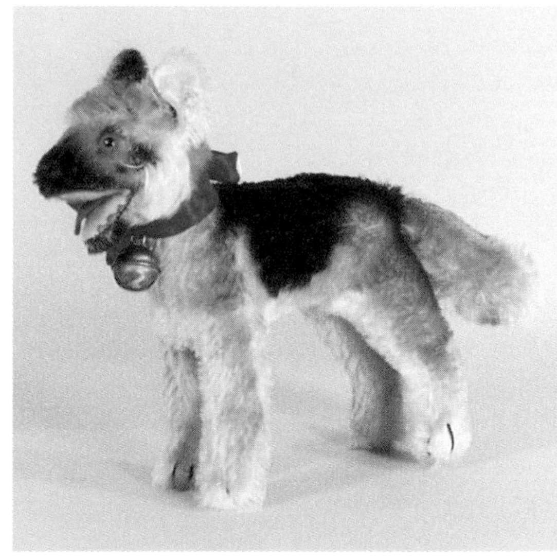

Steiff "Bernie" St. Bernard: 9in (23cm)
White and tan mohair; brown glass eyes; excelsior stuffed collar; near mint; hard to find in this large size.
MARKS: Raised button; chest tag
PRICE: $190

Steiff "Bernie" St. Bernard: 4in (10cm)
White and rusty brown mohair; brown glass eyes; excelsior stuffed; collar; near mint; rarer standing than sitting.
MARKS: Raised button
PRICE: $90

Steiff St. Bernard on Wheels: 20in (51cm)
White and rust mohair; brown glass eyes; excelsior stuffed; pull squeaker on back; rubber-tired metal wheels; wear on back; hard to find.
MARKS: U S Zone tag
PRICE: $300

Steiff "Dally" Dalmation: $6\frac{1}{2}$in (17cm)
White and blackish brown mohair; swivel head; excelsior stuffed; brown glass eyes; open felt-lined mouth; collar; excellent condition; somewhat hard to find.
MARKS: Raised button
PRICE: $150

Steiff "Electrola-Fox" (RCA) Dog: 7in (18cm)
Sheared white dralon with rust and brown markings; mohair ears; soft and hard stuffed; brown glass eyes; collar; mint condition; rare.
MARKS: Raised button; chest tag
PRICE: $550-up

Steiff "Bully" Dog: 8½in (22cm)
White, brown and black mohair; velvet muzzle; excelsior stuffed; brown glass eyes; collar; mint; rare this size.
MARKS: Raised button
PRICE: $160

Steiff "Beppo" Dog: 5in (13cm)

Tan and dark brown mohair; all jointed; excelsior stuffed; brown glass eyes; open mouth with tongue; collar; excellent condition; reasonably easy to find.

MARKS: Raised button

PRICE: $75

Steiff "Rolly" Dalmation: 7in (18cm)

Walt Disney Productions from *101 Dalmations*; white and black mohair; black and white plastic googly eyes backed with white oil cloth; excelsior stuffed; velvet nose; collar; mint; very rare.

MARKS: Raised button; chest tag

PRICE: $525

Steiff Pomeranian: 5in (13cm)
White woolly plush; velvet muzzle; brown glass eyes; excelsior stuffed; excellent condition; rare.
MARKS: Raised button
PRICE: $145

Steiff Chow: 5in (13cm)
Gold woolly plush; velvet muzzle; brown glass eyes; excelsior stuffed; tissue mint; somewhat rare.
MARKS: Raised button; chest tag
PRICE: $145

Steiff "Theophil" Dog: 6in (15cm)
Long shaggy dralon; mohair ears and whiskers; brown plastic eyes; excelsior stuffed. This was one of the animals (see "Ponx" tiger) that came in a cage box; excellent condition; somewhat rare.
MARKS: Incised button
PRICE: $75

Steiff Terrier: 6in (15cm)
Long silky tan mohair; brown glass eyes; excelsior stuffed; wire in ears. Much like earlier "Skye" terrier but without black markings. Excellent condition; rare.
MARKS: Raised button
PRICE: $95

Steiff "Scotty" Dog: 6in (15cm)

Black mohair; brown and white paperweight eyes; excelsior stuffed; collar; excellent condition; hard to find.

MARKS: Raised button; chest tag

PRICE: $190

Steiff "Cockie" Cocker Spaniel: 7in (18cm)

Black and white mohair; black and white eyes; excelsior stuffed; collar; near mint; somewhat easy to find — a great favorite.

MARKS: Raised button; chest tag

PRICE: $140

Steiff "Hoppel Dachel" Dog on Wheels: $11\frac{1}{8}$in (28cm)

Tan and brown mohair; open felt mouth with tongue; brown glass eyes; excelsior stuffed; rubber-tired red metal wheels; collar; this is "Lumpi" dog; tissue mint; rare. Rhino described elsewhere.

MARKS: Raised button; chest tag

PRICE: $400

Ruth Baum Collection.

Steiff "Waldili" Hunter Dachshund: 9in (23cm)
Rust mohair; brown glass eyes; hard stuffed; felt clothes; wooden rifle; tissue mint; somewhat hard to find.
MARKS: Incised button; chest tag
PRICE: $195-up

Steiff "Hucky" Crow: 7in (18cm)

Black mohair; black felt wings and tail; red felt open beak; black plastic eyes backed with red felt; red metal feet; swivel head; excelsior stuffed; tissue mint; common.

MARKS: Raised button; chest tag

PRICE: $100-up

Steiff "Gimpel" Finch: 4in (10cm)

Tan, orange and black mohair; black bead eyes; horsehair tail and wing tips; excelsior stuffed; clear plastic wrapped wire legs; tissue mint; rare. Rotation of one leg moves the alternate wing.

MARKS: Raised button; chest tag

PRICE: $225-up

Steiff "Wittie" Owl: 9in (23cm)

Varicolored mohair; felt wings and feet; green glass eyes; excelsior stuffed; tissue mint; owl common in all sizes.

MARKS: Incised button attached to wing; chest tag

PRICE: $95

Steiff Nesting Boxes: 3⅜in (9cm)

Wooden with round opening and perch for wool ball birds; one on right has money slot and Steiff paper sticker; both near mint; somewhat hard to find.

PRICE: $125-up

Steiff Wool Ball Duck: 2½in (6cm)

Multicolored wool; metal feet; near mint; easy to find.

MARKS: Raised button

PRICE: $35

Dennis Yusa Collection.

Steiff "Bluebonnet" Bird: 6½in (17cm)

Blue, white, yellow and black shaded mohair; blue felt wings and tail; black glass eyes; red metal feet; swivel head; excelsior stuffed; mint; rare size.

MARKS: Raised button; chest tag

PRICE: $225

Steiff "Tucky" Turkey: 4¾in (12cm)

Varicolored mohair; red velvet head; white and gray tail and wings; metal legs; excelsior stuffed; mint; somewhat rare.

MARKS: Raised button on tail; chest tag

PRICE: $165-up

Steiff "Piccy" Pelican: 6½in (17cm)
Shaded white mohair; felt beak (with plastic teeth) and feet; black and white glass eyes; excelsior stuffed; mint; hard to find.
MARKS: Raised button; chest tag
PRICE: $150-up

Steiff Floppy Hen: 6in (15cm)

White and gold flecked mohair; felt face, wattle and comb; soft stuffed; tissue mint. While most floppy animals are not popular, this proves the exception. Most beautifully colored and somewhat rare.

MARKS: Raised button; chest tag

PRICE: $145

Steiff Duck on Eccentric Wheels: $7\frac{1}{2}$in (19cm)

Varicolored mohair; felt beak and swimming positioned legs; excelsior stuffed; black plastic eyes; pull string attached to chest; excellent condition; reasonably easy to find.

MARKS: Chest tag

PRICE: $125

Steiff Penguins:

Left: 5¾in (15cm)
A circa 1950 copy of earlier one; white and black mohair with velvet flippers; red felt beak and feet; brown glass eyes; excelsior stuffed; somewhat rare.
MARKS: Raised button
PRICE: $110

Right: "Peggy" Penguin 8in (20cm)
White, black and gray mohair; red felt beak; tan felt feet; brown glass eyes; excelsior stuffed; mint; fairly common.
MARKS: Raised button; chest tag
PRICE: $80

Steiff "Swapl" Lamb: 8½in (22cm)
Curly black Persian lamb look to plush; mohair inset face; blue glass eyes; open pink velvet mouth; excelsior stuffed; near mint; this large size harder to find than small.
MARKS: Raised button
PRICE: $160-up

Steiff "Swapl" Lamb: 4in (10cm)

Black curly plush, white top knot; blue glass eyes; excelsior stuffed; felt ears; excellent condition; somewhat hard to find.

MARKS: Raised button; chest tag

PRICE: $95

Steiff "Bessy" Cow: 6in (15cm)

White and rust mohair; felt horns and udder; open felt-lined mouth; black and white plastic eyes; excelsior stuffed; collar; tissue mint; reasonably easy to find.

MARKS: Raised button; chest tag

PRICE: $155

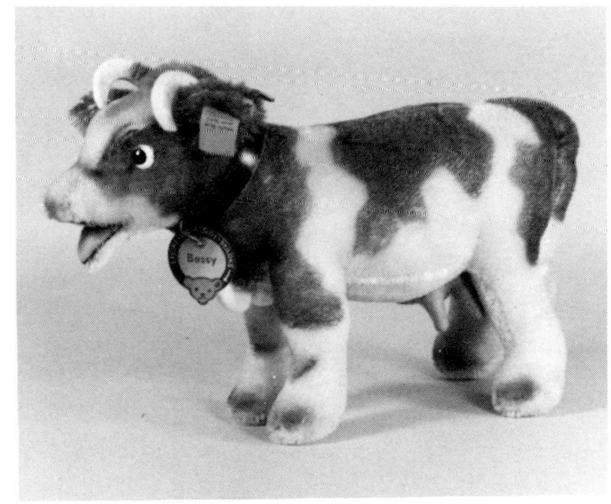

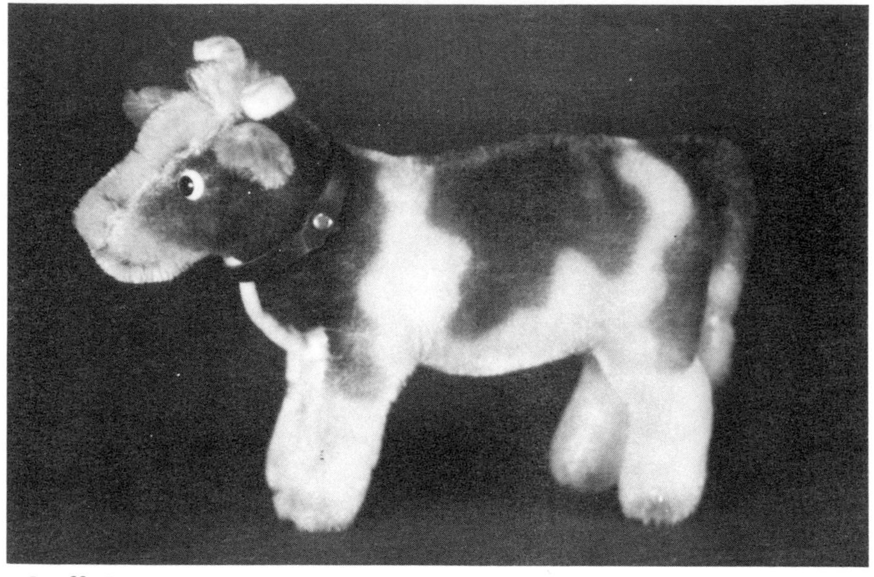

Steiff "Bessy" Cow: 5in (13cm)
The same as larger cow but without open mouth and udder. Circa 1960.
MARKS: No ID
PRICE: $75

Steiff "Oxy" Oxen:
Caramel mohair and velvet. Black and white glass eyes; excelsior stuffed; rope tail on small size; mint condition; rare.
4in (10cm)
MARKS: No ID
PRICE: $130 up
8⅝in (22cm)
MARKS: Raised button
PRICE: $625

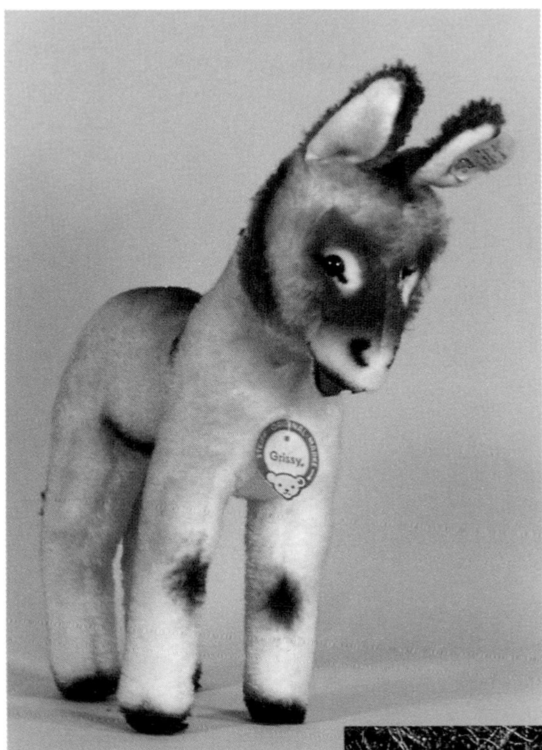

Steiff "Grissy" Donkey: 10in (25cm)

Varicolored dralon; black plastic eyes; soft and hard stuffed; open mouth; tissue mint; reasonably easy to find.

MARKS: Incised button; chest tag

PRICE: $85

Steiff Riding Horse on Wheels: 36in (91cm)

Largest size; brown, white and black mohair; brown glass eyes; saddle and bridle; excellent condition; rare size.

MARKS: Raised button; U S Zone tag

PRICE: $2000-up

Lorraine Oakley Condition.

Steiff Pig: 4in (10cm)
Pink velvet; blue glass eyes; soft and hard stuffed; felt ears; mint-in-bag.
MARKS: Incised button
PRICE: $65

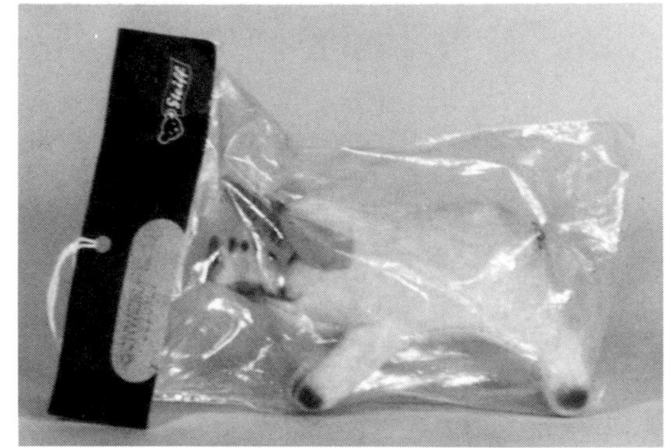

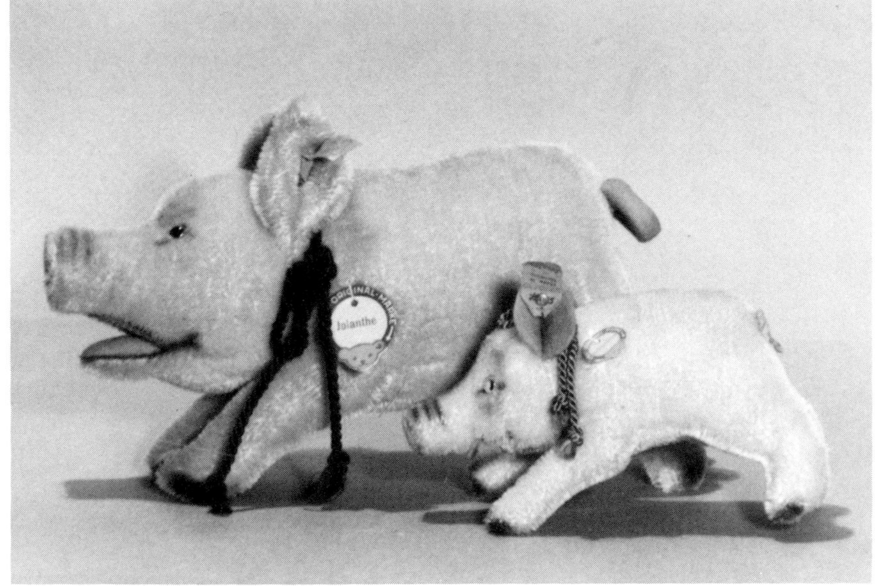

Steiff "Jolanthe" Pig: 8½in (22cm) long
Pink mohair; felt nose and tail; open felt-lined mouth; excelsior stuffed; blue glass eyes; red silk cord; mint; rare size.
MARKS: Raised button; chest tag
PRICE: $155

Steiff "Jolanthe" Pig: 5½in (14cm) long
Pink mohair; felt ears and bottom of mouth; cord tail; blue glass eyes; excelsior stuffed; green silk cord; mint; reasonably easy to find.
MARKS: Raised button; chest tag
PRICE: $80
Note the vast difference a few inches makes in over-all appearance.

Steiff "Zicky" Goat: 4in (10cm)
Shaded tan mohair; felt ears; green glass eyes; excelsior stuffed; ribbon and bell; mint; easy to find.
MARKS: Raised button; chest tag
PRICE: $65

Steiff Squirrel: 6in (15cm)
White brown tipped mohair; felt paws holding velvet acorn; black plastic eyes backed with felt; excelsior stuffed; nose is airbrushed and not embroidered as in most animals; mint; fairly common.
MARKS: Incised button.
PRICE: $45

Steiff Squirrel: 3½in (9cm)
Tan velvet; mohair tail; excelsior stuffed; black eyes; mint; hard to find.
MARKS: Raised button
PRICE: $55

Steiff Fawn: 5in (13cm)
Spotted tan velvet; excelsior stuffed; black eyes; excellent condition; hard to find. Circa 1955.
MARKS: No ID
PRICE: $45

Steiff Beaver 4in (10cm)
Tan mohair; felt tail; black and white plastic eyes; red tie; excelsior stuffed. Made for a Canadian airline. Excellent condition; rare.
MARKS: Raised button
PRICE: $95

Steiff "Raccy" Raccoon: 6in (15cm)

Tan marked mohair; brown glass eyes; excelsior stuffed; swivel head; excellent condition; somewhat hard to find.
MARKS: Raised button
PRICE: $95

Steiff "Piff" Groundhog: 7in (18cm)

Varicolored mohair; black plastic eyes; padded felt feet; double weight felt paws; open mouth; swivel head; excelsior stuffed; mint; somewhat hard to find. Circa 1965.
MARKS: Chest tag
PRICE: $130

Steiff Skunk: 4in (10cm)
Black velvet and white and black mohair; brown glass eyes; excelsior stuffed; tissue mint; somewhat rare.
MARKS: Raised button; chest tag
PRICE: $140

Steiff "Wiggy" Weasel: 8½in (22cm)
White dralon; black plastic eyes; soft stuffed; pipe cleaner tail; mint; hard to find. Also came in brown.
MARKS: Raised button; chest tag
PRICE: $90-up

Steiff "Dormy" Dormouse: 10in (25cm)
Beige and brown tipped mohair; black plastic eyes; soft stuffed; mint; somewhat hard to find.
MARKS: Incised button; chest tag
PRICE: $145

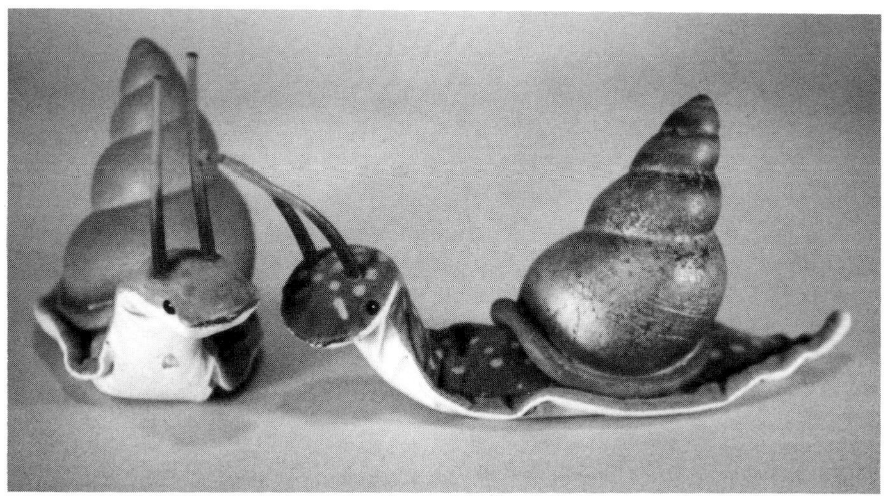

Steiff "Nelly" Snail: 6½in (17cm)
Green or brown velvet; white plastic under belly; iridescent shell; plastic eyes and antennae; near mint; brown rarer than green.
MARKS: Raised button
PRICE: $200

Steiff Rabbit: 7in (18cm)
Gold mohair; brown glass eyes; swivel head; nice contouring to haunches; excelsior stuffed; mint; somewhat hard to find.
MARKS: Raised button
PRICE: $85

Steiff Easter Bunny: 9in (23cm)
Tan mohair; brown glass eyes; excelsior stuffed; swivel head and arms; outsize feet; basket missing; near mint; hard to find.
MARKS: Raised button
PRICE: $125

Steiff "Niki" Rabbit: 12in (31cm)

Tan mohair; brown glass eyes; all jointed; very large felt feet; open mouth; excellent condition; large size somewhat rare.

MARKS: Raised button

PRICE: $225

Steiff "Sassy" Rabbit: 8½in (22cm)

Tan and white mohair; brown glass eyes; excelsior stuffed; swivel head; mint; somewhat hard to find.

MARKS: Raised button; chest tag

PRICE: $90-up

Deborah Pugliani Collection.

Steiff "Manni" Rabbits:
Tan shaded mohair; swivel head and arms; smaller has open felt-lined mouth; brown glass eyes; excelsior stuffed; near mint; rare sizes.
20in (51cm)
MARKS: Raised button
PRICE: $400-up
30in (76cm)
MARKS: Raised button; chest tag
PRICE: $650-up
Elaine Bosler Collection.

Steiff Dressed Rabbits:
24in (61cm)
Tan shaded mohair; open felt mouth; brown glass eyes; excelsior stuffed; swivel head and arms; felt and cotton clothes; baskets missing from back; near mint rare. Circa 1955.
MARKS: No ID
PRICE: $500-up each
Deborah Pugliani Collection.

Steiff "Lulac" Rabbits:

Tan and peach mohair; open felt mouth; long dangly limbs; felt foot pads; shaggy paws; blue and black glass crosseyes; soft and hard stuffed; mint; two largest sizes rare.

12in (31cm)
MARKS: Raised button; chest tag
PRICE: $150

30in (76cm) Display Rabbit
MARKS: Raised button; chest tag
PRICE: $650

20in (51cm). Circa 1960.
MARKS: No ID
PRICE: $300

Elaine Bosler Collection.

Steiff "Sonny" Rabbit: 3in (8cm)
Varicolored mohair; brown glass eyes; excelsior stuffed; swivel head; excellent condition; somewhat hard to find.
MARKS: Raised button
PRICE: $65

Steiff "Varlo" Rabbit: 7in (17cm)
Off-white mohair; brown glass eyes; excelsior stuffed; swivel head and back legs so can assume positions; not much contour to head so can appear flattish; mint; somewhat hard to find.
MARKS: Raised button; chest tag
PRICE: $90

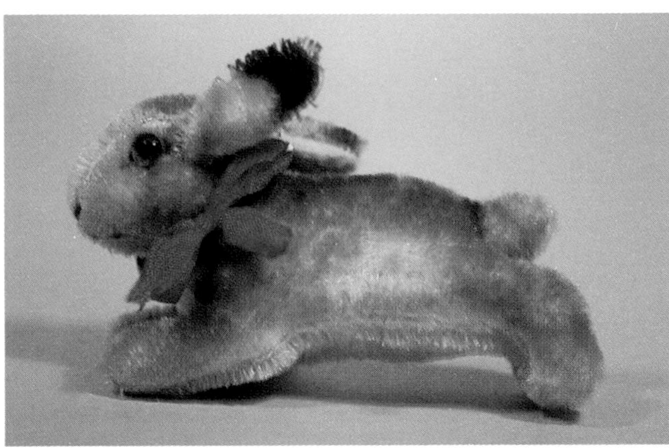

Steiff Bunny: 4½in (12cm)
Varicolored mohair; brown glass eyes; excelsior stuffed; ribbon and bell; excellent condition; reasonbly easy to find.
MARKS: U S Zone Germany
PRICE: $65

Steiff "Yella" Rabbit: 10in (25cm)
Pale yellow mohair; glass eyes; excelsior stuffed; swivel head; wide spread arms; stands on cardboard-lined feet; felt and cotton dress; excellent condition; rare.
MARKS: Raised button
PRICE: $200-up

Steiff "Ossili" Rabbit: 12in (31cm)
Tan mohair; white mohair feet; tan plastic soles; swivel head and arms; brown glass eyes; excelsior stuffed; open felt mouth; wearing green felt apron; excellent condition; somewhat easy to find.
MARKS: Raised button
PRICE: $105

Steiff "Hansili" Rabbits: 28in (71cm)
Tan shaded plush; brown glass eyes; swivel head and arms; excelsior stuffed; standing; finely detailed cotton and wool clothes; mint; rare.
MARKS: Raised buttons; chest tag on boy
PRICE: $700-up each. Add value for pair.
Mary Phillips Collection.

Steiff "Loopy" Wolf: 12in (31cm) by 14in (36cm)
Long and short tan mohair; open mouth with tongue and fangs; brown glass eyes; excelsior stuffed; near mint; very rare.
MARKS: Raised button; chest tag.
PRICE: $800-up

Steiff Cosy "Xorry" Fox: 12in (31cm)
Natural colored dralon; soft stuffed; embroidered sleep eyes; white thread across nose; near mint; somewhat hard to find.
MARKS: Raised button; chest tag
PRICE: $95
Barbara Chadwick Collection.

Steiff "Xorry" Fox: 10in (25cm)
Orange mohair; black mohair back of ears; brown glass eyes; excelsior stuffed; mint; common except in this largest size which is rare.
MARKS: Raised button
PRICE: $220

Steiff Fox: 3½in (9cm)
Orange mohair; brown glass eyes; excelsior stuffed; mint; while small Xorry is common, this fox is rare.
MARKS: Raised button
PRICE: $90

Steiff Lynx: 7in (18cm)
Tan and white mohair; brilliant orange plastic eyes; black horsehair ear tufts; mint; somewhat rare.
MARKS: Raised button
PRICE: $225

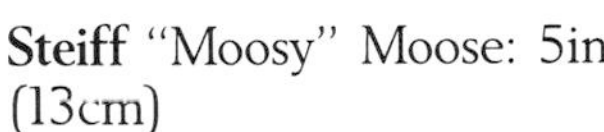

Steiff "Moosy" Moose: 5in (13cm)
Brown and white mohair; felt antlers; black glass eyes; excelsior stuffed; tissue mint; hard to find.
MARKS: Raised button; chest tag
PRICE: $200

Steiff "Renny" Reindeer: 11in (28cm)

White, tan and brown mohair; brown glass eyes; felt-covered wire antlers; excelsior stuffed; stitch on nose; mint; larger size harder to find.

MARKS: Incised button; chest tag

PRICE: $165-up

Steiff College Dressed Animals:

Princeton Tiger: 14in (36cm)
MARKS: Raised button
PRICE: $700

Navy Goat: 12in (31cm)
MARKS: Raised button
PRICE: $550

Yale Bully: 12in (31cm)
MARKS: Raised button
PRICE: $450

Natural colored mohair; green glass eyes; excelsior stuffed; all are hard-to-find sizes; rare with the blankets.

Michelle Daunton Collection.

Steiff "Pandy" Lesser Panda: 4in (10cm)
White, orange and black mohair; brown glass eyes; swivel head; excelsior stuffed; excellent condition; somewhat rare — especially larger one.
MARKS: Raised button
PRICE: $200-up

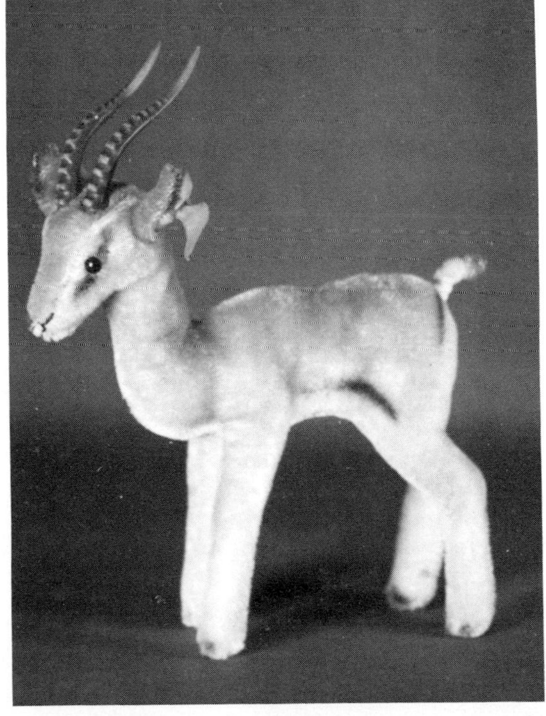

Steiff "Yuku" Gazelle: 8½in (22cm) plus antlers
Tan and gold mohair; black plastic eyes; excelsior stuffed; rubber antlers; mint; somewhat rare.
MARKS: Raised button
PRICE: $160-up

Steiff Mini Lion Family:

"Leo": 4in (10cm)

Tan and brown mohair; brown glass eyes; excelsior stuffed; mint; reasonably easy to find.

MARKS: Raised button; chest tag

PRICE: $75

"Lea": 3½in (9cm)

Tan and brown mohair; brown glass eyes; excelsior stuffed; mint; hard to find.

MARKS: Raised button; chest tag

PRICE: $80

Cub: 3½in (9cm)

Tan mohair with spots; brown glass eyes; excelsior stuffed; swivel head; mint; reasonably easy to find.

MARKS: Chest tag

PRICE: $75

Steiff Papa Lion: 5½in (14cm)

Tan mohair with long tipped mane; gold glass eyes; all jointed; excelsior stuffed; mint; somewhat hard to find.

MARKS: Chest tag

PRICE: $125

Steiff Lion Cub: 6in (15cm)
Spotted tan mohair; brown glass eyes; swivel head; excelsior stuffed; excellent condition; hard to find.
MARKS: Raised button
PRICE: $165

Steiff Mama Lion: 8½in (22cm)
Gold mohair; brown glass eyes; all jointed; excelsior stuffed; excellent condition; somewhat rare.
MARKS: Raised button
PRICE: $250

Steiff Tiger: 5in (13cm)
Tan, gold and black striped mohair; green glass eyes; excelsior stuffed; all jointed; mint; somewhat hard to find; shown with box from circa 1960.
MARKS: Raised button
PRICE: $125

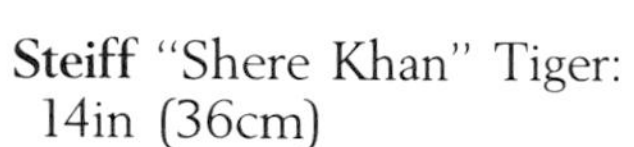

Steiff "Shere Khan" Tiger: 14in (36cm)
Walt Disney Productions; orange, white and black dralon; green glass eyes; soft and hard stuffed; excellent condition; rare.
MARKS: Raised button; chest tag
PRICE: $300

Steiff Jungle Book Animals:

"Baby Hathi" Elephant: 8in (20cm)

Gray plush; open felt mouth and ears; plush top knot; black and white eyes; soft and hard stuffed; mint; easiest to find of the quartet.

MARKS: Incised button

PRICE: $95

"King Louie" Ape: 10in (25cm)

Brown and orange plush; orange long headpiece; description same as above, mint; somewhat hard to find.

MARKS: Incised button

PRICE: $105

"Baloo" Bear: 16in (41cm)

Brown and tan plush; description same as above; mint; hardest to find of all.

MARKS: Incised button

PRICE: $250

"Shere Khan" described elsewhere.

Ruth Baum Collection.

Steiff "Ponx" Tiger-in-Cage Box: 7in (18cm)
Varicolored dralon; green plastic eyes; soft and hard stuffed; tissue mint; rare to find so complete.
MARK: Incised button; chest tag; presentation box and booklet
PRICE: $125

Steiff Reclining Leopard: 10in (25cm)
Tan, orange and black spotted mohair; green glass eyes; ear tufts; soft and hard stuffed; mint; somewhat easy to find.
MARKS: U S Zone tag
PRICE: $105

Steiff Leopard: 10in (25cm)
Steiff Ocelot: 9in (23cm)

The ocelot compared to the leopard is paler in color, has no ear tufts and has orange eyes instead of green. In the absence of the chest tags, these points should be noted for identification.
MARKS: Raised button; chest tag
PRICE: $155

Steiff Gibbon: 6in (18cm)

Shaded tan mohair; black felt palms; black and white glass eyes; excelsior stuffed; very long arms; mint; hard to find.
MARKS: Raised button
PRICE: $120

Steiff "Coco" Babboon: 6in (15cm)
Gray mohair; felt inset face; felt ears and paws; excelsior stuffed; collar; green glass eyes; swivel head; tissue mint; somewhat easy to find.
MARKS: Raised button; chest tag
PRICE: $95

Steiff "Coco" Babboon: 12in (31cm)
Gray mohair; felt inset face; felt paws and ears; horsehair mantle; brown glass eyes set in lids; excelsior stuffed; all jointed; excellent condition; very rare in this size.
MARKS: Chest tag
PRICE: $295-up

Steiff Dangling Orangutan: 22in (56cm) arm span
Long rust fur; jersey paws; rubber face; soft loosely stuffed; tissue mint; rare.
MARKS: Raised button; chest tag
PRICE: $145

Steiff "Cocoli" Monkey: 4in (10cm)

Felt face surrounded by mohair; black velvet back of head; rubber body; green glass eyes; felt and cotton clothes not removable; mint; rare.

MARKS: Raised button; chest tag

PRICE: $140-up

Deborah Pugliani Collection.

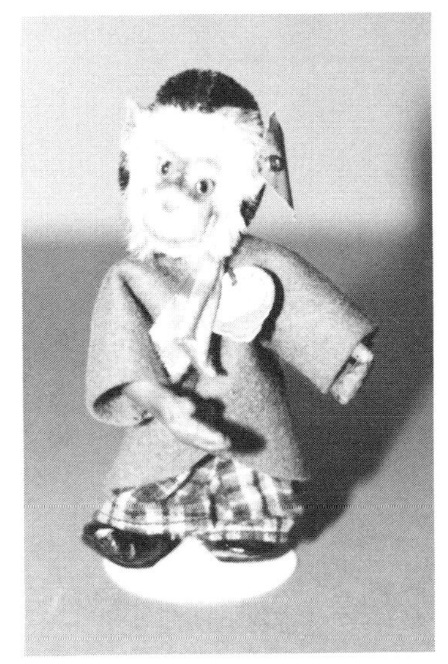

Steiff "Jocko" Monkey: 13½in (34cm) sitting

Brown curly mohair; felt face, ears and paws; brown glass eyes set in lids; all jointed; mint. Common except in this size and largest.

MARKS: Raised button

PRICE: $105

Steiff "Nosy" Rhino: 7in (18cm)
Gray airbrushed mohair; black and white plastic eyes; felt ears and horn; soft and hard stuffed; tissue mint; "Nosy" fairly common but all animals in this condition desirable.
MARKS: Incised button; chest tag
PRICE: $90

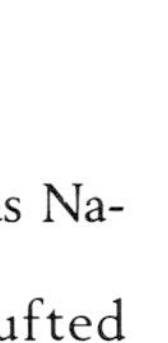

Steiff "Rheinhold Das Nashorn": 9in (23cm)
Gray mohair; tufted crown; felt horn; leather-like pads; black and white plastic eyes; swivel head and arms; soft and hard stuffed; character from German magazine; mint; very rare.
MARKS: Raised button
PRICE: $325-up

Steiff Zebra: 10in (25cm)
Blackish brown on white mohair; black felt hooves; brown glass eyes; excelsior stuffed; Zebras not rare but this one especially nice; mint.
MARKS: Raised button; chest tag
PRICE: $130

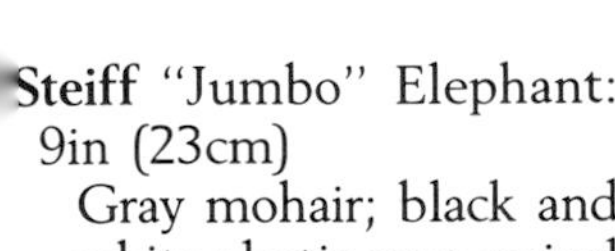

Steiff "Jumbo" Elephant: 9in (23cm)
Gray mohair; black and white plastic eyes; swivel head and arms; soft stuffed; felt pads; upright trunk with bell; red felt bib; mint; somewhat hard to find.
MARKS: Incised button
PRICE: $125

Steiff "Snuggy Jumbo": 22in (56cm)
Gray mohair; black and white glass eyes; felt tusks; plastic soles; excelsior stuffed; red felt blanket; excellent condition; rare.
MARKS: Raised button
PRICE: $500

Steiff "Spidy" 9in (23cm)
Varicolored mohair; mohair covered wire legs (small one has pipe cleaner legs); 7 black bead eyes; tissue mint; rare.
MARKS: Raised button on leg; chest tag
PRICE: $750

Steiff "Eric" Bat: 12in (31cm) wing span
Tan and off-white mohair; double felt ears; limbs are wire covered mohair; black glass bead eyes and nose; iridescent plastic wings; mint; rare. rare.
MARKS: Raised button; chest tag
PRICE: $750

"Eric" Bat: 8in (20cm) wing span
Tan and off-white mohair; double felt ears; pipe cleaner limbs; black glass bead eyes and nose; iridescent; plastic wings, mint; rare.
MARKS: Raised button
PRICE: $325

Steiff "Crabby" Lobster: 12in (31cm)
Gold, orange and red mohair; orange wire-covered chenille legs; black glass eyes; long red cord feelers; excelsior stuffed; mint; very rare to find in mohair.
MARKS: Raised button
PRICE: $525

RIGHT: **Steiff Dinosaurs**

"Brosus": 12in (31cm)
Varicolored mohair; green and black glass eyes; orange felt spines; excelsior stuffed; tissue mint; rare.
MARKS: Raised button; chest tag
PRICE: $1000-up

"Tysus": 8in (20cm)
Varicolored mohair; black and white glass eyes; swivel arms; excelsior stuffed; open mouth; green felt spines; tisssue mint; rare.
MARKS: Raised button; chest tag
PRICE: $1000-up

"Dinos": 12in (31cm)
Varicolored mohair; green and black glass eyes; excelsior stuffed; open mouth; two rows of blue and pink felt spines; tissue mint; rare.
MARKS: Raised button; chest tag
PRICE: $1000-up

Steiff "Roloplan" Kite
Cotton with wooden dowels. Comes in bag; mint; rare.
MARKS: Imprinted with Steiff logo and bear's head. Both kite and carrying bag have raised buttons on the bear's head.
PRICE: $150-up

Steiff "Tysus" Dinosaur: 17in (43cm)

Tan, brown and green marked mohair; black and white glass eyes; excelsior stuffed; felt spines; open felt lined mouth; swivel arms; mint; rare. Circa 1955.
MARKS: Chest tag
PRICE: $1200-up
Deborah Pugliani Collection.

Steiff "Dinos"" Dinosaur: 31in (79cm)
Gold, green and red marked mohair; glass eyes; open felt mouth; excelsior stuffed; mint; rare. Circa 1955.
MARKS: Chest tag
PRICE: $1500
Deborah Pugliani Collection.

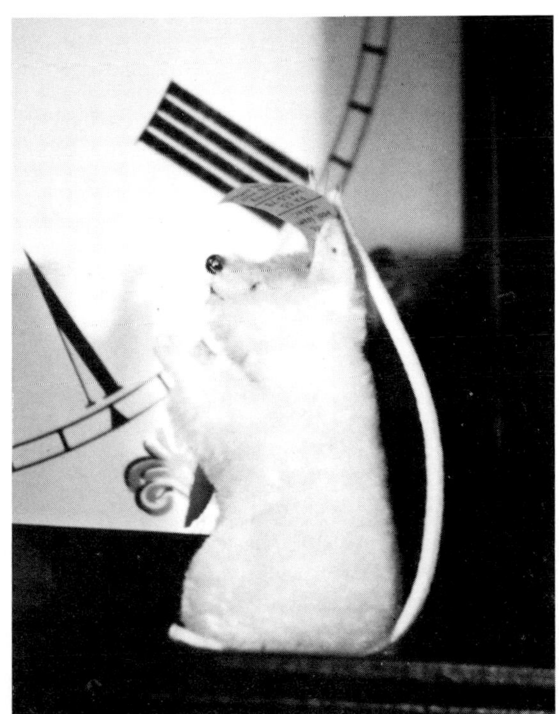

Steiff "Pieps" Mouse: 3½in (12cm)
White mohair; felt feet and tail; pink bead eyes; black bead nose; excelsior stuffed; also came in gray with black eyes (white more common); tissue mint; easy to find.
MARKS: Raised button; chest tag
PRICE: $60

Steiff City and Country Mice:

In the 1950s and early 1960s F.A.O. Schwarz (and other stores) equipped Steiff toys in many charming ways. Using "Pieps" mice, they had 7in (18cm) by 13in (33cm) by 4½in (14cm) wooden houses built for them. The city mouse is white and dressed in blue satin and velvet. Her house is a Georgian brick and opens to reveal an elegant interior. A red velvet canopy bed complete with bolster and gilt accessories against a gold striped wall paper carry out the theme. The country mouse is the less common gray color and her home is rustic. There is even a round hole in back for quick exits. Her apron is gingham and she is prepared for work with a variety of cleaning and cooking supplies. There is a ladder to a bunk bed and other wooden furniture; very rare.

MARKS: F.A.O. Schwarz sticker on each house.

PRICE: $350-up each — depending on completeness

Steiff "Cappy" Doll: 11in (28cm)
Rubber head; painted features; black wig; felt bendable body; red and blue rayon clown suit; felt hat and shoes; brass bells; excellent condition; reasonably easy to find.
MARKS: Raised button on wrist bracelet; chest tag
PRICE: $125

Steiff "Sandy" doll: 11in (28cm)
Same mold and description as "Cappy;" felt clothes decorated with gold stars and ruff; gray hair; carries a cotton bag; supposed to be the sandman; near mint; harder to find than "Cappy."
MARKS: Raised button on wrist bracelet
PRICE: $125

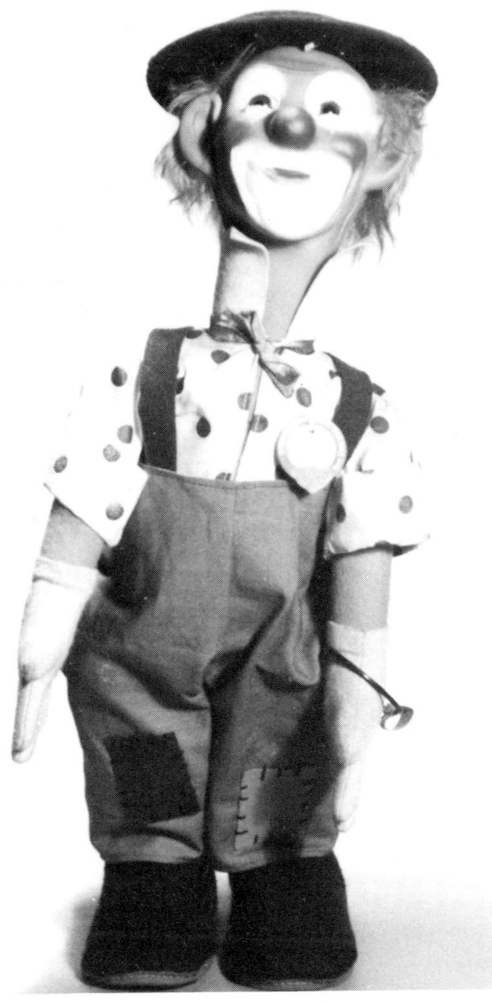

Steiff "Clownie": 17in (43cm)

Rubber painted face; inset glass eyes; jointed felt body; felt and cotton clothes; near mint; rare in this size; quite magnificent as compared to smaller sizes.

MARKS: Raised button on wrist bracelet; chest tag

PRICE: $350

Steiff "Tele Maxl" Doll: 12in (31cm)
Rubber head; felt body; cotton and felt clothes; made especially for TV company in Munich; mint; not found in United States.
MARKS: Chest tag
PRICE: $175
Ruth Baum Collection.

Steiff "Alpa" and "Alpo": 4in (10cm)
Tyro dressed hedgehogs; hard rubber-like bodies; felt and cotton clothes; tissue mint; somewhat rare.
MARKS: Raised button secured by stock tag around ankle; chest tag
PRICE: $95-up each

ABOVE:
Steiff "Gucki," "Lucki" and "Pucki" 12in (31cm)
All-jointed felt bodies; rubber faces with painted eyes and mohair wigs and beards; felt and cotton clothes; feathers on hats secured by Steiff buttons; common in small size; relatively rare in this size; excellent condition.
MARKS: Raised button on plastic bracelet; chest tag
PRICE: $150-up each

LEFT:
Steiff "Mecki" Dressed Hedgehog: 11in (28cm)
Rubber body; mohair wig; painted features; cotton and felt clothes; swivel head; excellent condition; easy to find.
MARKS: Raised button; chest tag
PRICE: $90
Deborah Pugliani Collection.

Steiff Studio Basset: 25in 64cm)
Tan and brown shaded mohair; excelsior stuffed; large wooden eyes; needs some repair; rare. Circa 1955.
MARKS: No ID
PRICE: $650
Dennis Yusa Collection.

Steiff "Electrola Fox" Studio Dog: 19⅝in (50cm)
White, rust and brown sheared dralon; mohair ears; brown glass eyes; excelsior stuffed; near mint; rare.
MARKS: Raised button
PRICE: $1000
Ruth Baum Collection.

Steiff "Teddy-Baby" Studio Teddy: 60in (152cm)
Long brown curly mohair; tan sheared snout; open felt-lined mouth; felt pads; leather tops to feet; felt paw pads; glass eyes; excelsior stuffed; all jointed; near mint; rare. Circa 1950.
MARKS: No ID
PRICE: $4000-up
Elaine Bosler Collection.

Steiff "Dally" Studio Dalmation: 27in (67cm)
White and black spotted mohair; open felt mouth; excelsior stuffed; swivel head; collar; near mint; rare.
MARKS: Raised button; chest tag
PRICE: $600-up
Elaine Bosler Collection

Steiff "Adebar" Studio Stork: 27in (67cm)
White, blue and black felt; orange reinforced felt open beak and feet; brown glass eyes; excelsior stuffed; tissue mint; rare.
MARKS: Raised button; chest tag
PRICE: $800
Michelle Daunton Collection.

Steiff Studio Buzzard: approximately 32in (81cm)
Natural colored mohair; rubber beak and claws; excelsior stuffed; brown glass eyes; mint; limited production.
MARKS: Raised button; hand-lettered tag.
PRICE: $1700-up

Steiff Studio Pterodactyl: 120in (305cm) wing span
Tan and red mohair; open leatherette beak and claws; green glass eyes; excelsior stuffed; mint; very rare.
MARKS: Raised button
PRICE: $4000
Elaine Bosler Collection

Steiff Studio "Dinos" Dinosaur: 120in (305cm)
Multicolored mohair; open mouth with red tongue; brown glass eyes; jointed at neck; fang; rubber claws; mint; very rare.
MARKS: Raised button
PRICE: $2500-up
Michelle Daunton Collection.

Steiff Studio Elephant: approximately 32in (81cm)
Gray mohair; black glass; excelsior stuffed; wooden tusks; mint; rare.
MARKS: Raised button
PRICE: No price available

Steiff Studio "Ely" Elephant: 40in (102cm)
Gray mohair; leatherette pads; glass eyes; swivel head and arms; upright trunk; excelsior stuffed; red felt bib; appears to be forerunner of "Jumbo;" mint; rare.
MARKS: Raised button; chest tag
PRICE: $1000-up
Elaine Bosler Collection.

Steiff "Jocko" Monkey: 32in (81cm)
Brown curly mohair; felt face, hands and feet; brown glass eyes set in lids; excelsior stuffed; all jointed; excellent condition; very rare size.
MARKS: Raised button
PRICE: $500-up
Lorraine Oakley Collection.

Steiff Bengal Tiger: 27in (67cm)
Natural colored striped mohair; green glass eyes; open felt-lined mouth with plastic fangs; excelsior stuffed; mint; rare.
MARKS: Raised button
PRICE: $600-up
Elaine Bosler Collection.

Steiff Studio Fox: 21½in (55cm)
Rust and white mohair; black back of paws; open felt mouth with tongue; missing teeth; excelsior stuffed; brown glass eyes; swivel head; near mint; rare. Circa 1955.
MARKS: No ID
PRICE: $750-up

Steiff Studio Female Fawn: 60in (152cm)

Tan spotted mohair; brown glass eyes; excelsior stuffed; wonderful innocent expression; near mint; rare.

MARKS: Raised button

PRICE: $1500

Michelle Daunton Collection.

Steiff Studio Boar: 31½in (80cm) high

Gray tipped mohair; open mouth; rubber tusks; excelsior stuffed; glass eyes; tissue mint; rare.

MARKS: Incised button; chest tag

PRICE: $1200-up

Lorraine Oakley Collection.

Steiff Studio Wolf (or Polar Dog): 27in (67cm)
Long tan mohair; sheared mohair muzzle, ears and legs; brown glass eyes; open mouth (fangs appear missing); excelsior stuffed; mint; rare.
MARKS: Raised button
PRICE: $1200 - up
Michelle Daunton Collection.

Steiff Boar: 15¾in (40cm)
Tan spotted mohair; open felt-lined mouth; glass eyes; excelsior stuffed; near mint; rare.
MARKS: Raised button; chest tag
PRICE: $750

Steiff Studio Goose: 24in (60cm)
White and brown marked mohair; open felt beak and feet; glass eyes; excelsior stuffed; mint; rare.
MARKS: Raised button; chest tag
PRICE: $900-up
Ruth Baum Collection.

Steiff Wooden Dog on Wheels: 6in (15cm)
Wood burned and varnished; red wheels; pull string; excellent condition; somewhat hard to find.
MARKS: Metal plaque on side
PRICE: $85

Steiff Wooden Camel on Wheels: 8in (20cm)
Same description as dog; mint; somewhat hard to find.
MARKS: Metal plaque on side
PRICE: $130
A variety of wooden pull toys were made; circa 1970.

Schuco Teddy Bears and Animals

There are many misconceptions regarding the dating of Schuco products. It is always assumed that perfume bottles and applied felt feet monkeys and bears are from the 1920-1930 era. In fact, they were produced in the postwar period as well. If this is the case, then how does one accurately date? Well, of course, no one is perfect, but there are some clues to help. On the issue of the small metal-faced monkey with applied feet, the metal on the face is very smooth and quite highly painted. Earlier examples are rougher textured and although metal, give the appearance of clay.

The perfume bottle is going to prove a little more difficult, except in one instance. At this time, both glass and plastic bottles were employed. The plastic bottle was meant to hold small candies referred to as "hundreds and thousands." Obviously, to find either a monkey or Teddy Bear containing a plastic vial will be of immeasurable help.

The bear perfume will cause a little more confusion. In general, the toys from the late 1940s and early 1950s can often be found in pristine condition. So let us assume that if you find such a perfume bear, gold in color and absolutely mint, the chances are greater that it is a later example.

"Tricky" dwarf and "Tricky" Father Christmas both wear eyeglasses. I expect that if one were found without the zone tag present, one would assume it was much earlier because the glasses were thought to be of a much earlier era.

The bottom line is to reiterate how difficult absolute dating is and in many cases should be avoided.

Schuco Identification Marks

The Schuco company, also of West Germany, identified this area, after the war, with a zone tag, also. I have only seen this on their "yes/no" toys but that is not to say a different form was not used on other items. If not removed (and this can perhaps be determined by a thread remaining on the left chest), it is very durable. Made of red plastic, it reads, "Schuco/Tricky/Patent/Ang." on the front and "D.B. Pat. Ang./Int. Patents/pending/Made in US-Zone/Germany" on the reverse.

The mechanism to cause the head to nod "yes" or shake "no" is metal and operated by levering the tail. Most of the products are mohair and excelsior stuffed. Those items 5in (13cm) or smaller have the covering directly over the metal and so are very hard to the touch. This enduring feature was used for many years and surely a supreme example of the toy maker's art.

Except for the bellhop bear, Teddy Bears from the 1950s are more in demand than their earlier bears. They possess wonderfully wistful faces, have downward-turned paws and the 8in (20cm) or larger sizes have cardboard-lined feet to facilitate standing. The eyes are usually clear glass or clear glass painted brown on the back.

The later toys have paper tags labeled "Bigo Bello" or "Heigi." They are triangular in shape and normally attached to the chest or wrist. Mohair was used on the bendable wire products, but eventually abandoned in favor of plush.

Schuco catalog, circa 1950.

the original **Schuco TRICKY** *head movement*

SCHUCO "TRICKY" ANIMALS

(with removable clothes)

Schuco "Tricky" Bear as Dutch boy or girl

Schuco "Tricky" Bear as Tyrolean boy or girl

Schuco "Tricky" Kitten

(clothes not removable)

Schuco "Tricky" Bunny

Schuco "Tricky" Kitten

Schuco "Tricky" Bear as dandy

SCHUCO "MOLLY" BEARS *with the soft as satin foam-rubber filling*

Anyone handling these SCHUCO "MOLLY" bears with their soft, pliable foam-rubber filling just once is immediately captivated. Correctly held and manipulated they turn and twist amusingly and even dance making highly original arm and leg movements. All animals in this range are made of moth-proof and high-class wool plush.

white, blond, red-brown, rose and light blue

brown fleeced plush

SCHUCO "ROLLY" PATENT

No. 7401 Acrobat — No. 7402 Monkey — No. 7403 Bear — No. 7404 Bunny

SCHUCO "ACROBAT"

Tumbling Bear made completely of best plush

Tumbling Caricature Mouse

Tumbling Tow-headed Peter made of felt

Tumbling Monkeys made of felt

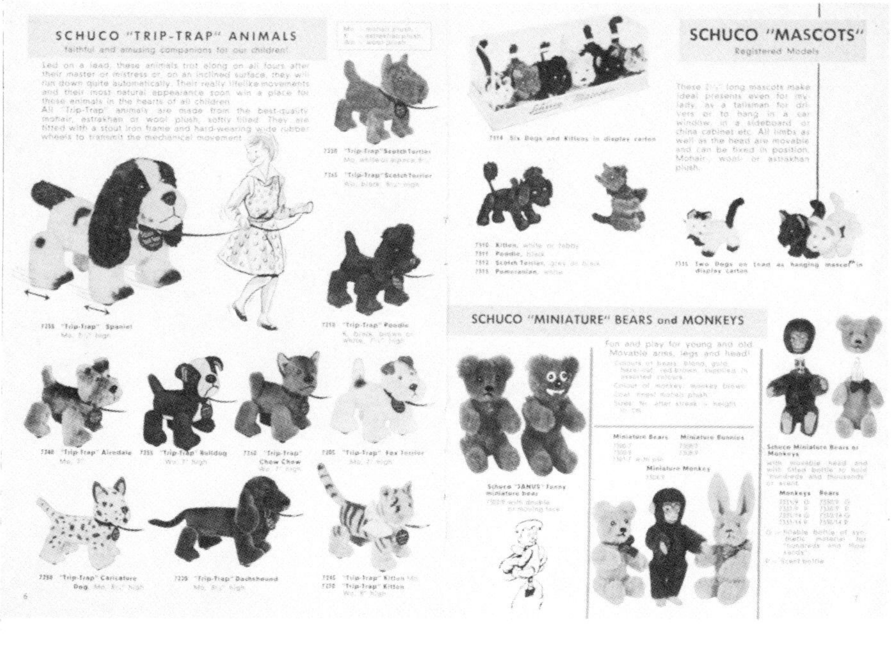

SCHUCO "TRIP-TRAP" ANIMALS

faithful and amusing companions for our children!

Led on a lead, these animals trot along on all fours after their master or mistress or, on an inclined surface, they will run down quite automatically. Their really lifelike movements and their most natural appearance soon win a place for those animals in the hearts of all children.

All "Trip-Trap" animals are made from the best-quality mohair, estrakhan or wool plush, softly filled. They are fitted with a stout iron frame and hard-wearing wide rubber wheels to transmit the mechanical movement.

7230 "Trip-Trap" Scotch Terrier

7245 "Trip-Trap" Scotch Terrier

7255 "Trip-Trap" Spaniel

7210 "Trip-Trap" Poodle

7240 "Trip-Trap" Airedale

7255 "Trip-Trap" Bulldog

7260 "Trip-Trap" Chow Chow

7205 "Trip-Trap" Fox Terrier

7250 "Trip-Trap" Caricature Dog

7220 "Trip-Trap" Dachshound

7265 "Trip-Trap" Kitten

7270 "Trip-Trap" Kitten

6

7314 Six Dogs and Kittens in display carton

SCHUCO "MASCOTS"

Registered Models

These long mascots make ideal presents even for my lady, as a talisman for drivers or to hang in a car window, in a sideboard or china cabinet etc. All limbs as well as the head are movable and can be fixed in position. Mohair, wool or astrakhan plush.

7310 Kitten, white or tabby

7311 Poodle, black

7312 Scotch Terrier, grey or black

7313 Pomeranian, white

7315 Two Dogs on lead as hanging mascot in display carton

SCHUCO "MINIATURE" BEARS and MONKEYS

Fun and play for young and old. Movable arms, legs and head!

Schuco "JANUS" funny miniature bear

with double or moving face

Miniature Bears — Miniature Bunnies

Miniature Monkey

Schuco Miniature Bears or Monkeys

with movable head and with filled bottle to hold "hundreds and thousands" or scent

Monkeys — Bears

R = Scent bottle

7

Schuco Yes/no Teddy Bear: 13in (33cm)

Pale beige mohair; brown glass eyes; excelsior stuffed; felt pads (split at cardboard sides on feet; common); excellent condition; somewhat hard to find.

MARKS: "Tricky" tag

PRICE: $700-up

Schuco Yes/no Teddy Bear: 13in (36cm)

Tan mohair head, paws and feet; cotton body, arms and legs; felt pads; brown glass eyes; excelsior stuffed; all jointed; orange print dress; green cotton apron; excellent condition; rare to find dressed bear. Circa 1950.
MARKS: No ID
PRICE: $1000

Schuco Yes/no Teddy Bear: 21⅝in (55cm)
Light brown mohair; tan felt pads; brown glass eyes; excelsior stuffed; all jointed; mint; rare size.
MARKS: "Tricky" tag
PRICE: $1200-up
Ruth Baum Collection.

Schuco Yes/no Teddy Bear: 12in (31cm)
Beige mohair; felt pads (repaired); clear glass eyes; excelsior stuffed; all jointed; fur off tail and some mohair wear; clothes not original; hard to find. 1953.
MARKS: No ID
PRICE: $450-up

Schuco Yes/no Teddy Bear: 7½in (19cm)
Beige mohair; felt pads (cardboard lined); clear glass eyes painted brown on back; excelsior stuffed; all jointed; excellent condition; hard to find.
MARKS: "Tricky" tag
PRICE: $500

Schuco Yes/no Teddy Bear: 14in (36cm)
Beige mohair; felt pads (cardboard lined); clear glass eyes; excelsior stuffed; all jointed; near mint; hard to find. Circa 1955.
MARKS: No ID
PRICE: $800-up

Schuco Yes/no Teddy Bear: 20in (51cm)

Beige mohair; clear eyes painted brown on back; felt pads; excelsior stuffed; all jointed; fur off tail — otherwise excellent; large size harder to find. Circa 1948.

MARKS: No ID

PRICE: $1100-up

Schuco Yes/no Teddy Bear: 16in (41cm)

Beige mohair; clear eyes painted brown on back; felt pads (cardboard lined); excelsior stuffed; all jointed; plastic nose. Music box plays German folk songs. A variety of songs were used, even "Oh My Papa!" Also came with embroidered nose. Fur sparse around music box ring. Split on side of soles (often found in bears with cardboard lining). Otherwise excellent; hard to find and in demand. Circa 1955.

MARKS: No ID

PRICE: $900-up

Schuco Yes/no Teddy Bear: 5in (13cm)
White mohair-over-metal; all jointed; brown glass eyes; red felt tongue; collar not original; near mint; rare color. Circa 1955.
MARKS: No ID
PRICE: $350-up

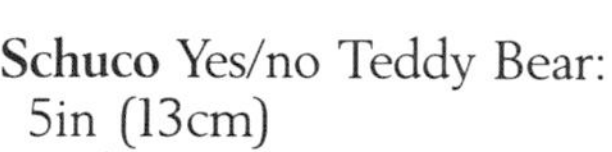

Schuco Yes/no Teddy Bear: 5in (13cm)
Black mohair-over-metal; all jointed; brown glass eyes; red felt tongue; gold foil crown; Berlin ribbon banner; mint; rare with crown and banner. Circa 1959.
MARKS: No ID
PRICE: $500-up

Schuco Yes/no Teddy Bear: 13in (33cm)

Caramel mohair; brown glass eyes; excelsior stuffed; felt pads; mint-in-box; rare to find with box.

MARKS: "Tricky" tag

PRICE: $1100

Ruth Baum Collection.

Schuco Yes/no Teddy Bear: 14in (36cm)
Pinky tan mohair; glass eyes; felt pads; excelsior stuffed; all jointed; acute downward bend to paws; tissue mint; rare to find perfection.
MARKS: "Tricky" tag
PRICE: $1000-up

Schuco "Musical" Yes/no Teddy Bear: 20in (51cm)
Pinky tan mohair; felt pads with bottom cardboard lined; clear glass eyes; excelsior stuffed; all jointed; bellows music box; mint; rare. Circa 1950.
MARKS: No ID
PRICE: $1800-up
Elaine Bosler Collection.

Schuco "Berlin" Teddy Bear: 3in (8cm)
Cinnamon mohair-over-metal; black bead eyes; all jointed; Berlin banner and gold metal crown; mint; hard to find. Circa 1955.
MARKS: No ID
PRICE: $175
Schuco "Berlin" Teddy Bear: 3in (8cm)
Brown mohair; same description as other.
Schuco Teddy Bear: 3in (8cm)
Gold mohair-over-metal; all jointed. Circa 1955.
MARKS: No ID
PRICE: $125
Retha Lourens Collection.

Schuco Yes/no Panda: 13in (33cm)
White and black mohair; cardboard-lined felt feet; glass eyes; felt tongue; all jointed; mint; hard to find. Circa 1955.
MARKS: No ID
PRICE: $1100

Schuco Yes/no Panda: 5in (13cm)
Black and white mohair over metal; glass eyes; all jointed; excellent condition; hard to find. Circa 1950.
MARKS: No ID
PRICE: $550

Lorraine Oakley Collection.

Schuco Standing Bear: 5½in (14cm)
Tan mohair head and arms; brown glass eyes; wired body; felt and rayon clothes not removable; plastic shoes; excellent condition; rare.
MARKS: On bottom of shoes "Int. Pat. Pend./D.B.G. M/original bigo fix/D.B. Patent Ang."
PRICE: $195-up

Schuco Teddy Bear: 2⅝in (7cm)
Gold mohair-over-metal; bead eyes; all jointed; near mint; somewhat easy to find. Circa 1960.
MARKS: No ID
PRICE: $125

Barbara Chadwick and Dennis Yusa Collection.

Schuco Teddy Bear: 3½in (9cm)
Rust mohair-over-metal; black bead eyes; applied felt feet; all jointed; mint; hard to find. Most likely circa 1950.
MARKS: No ID
PRICE: $150

Schuco Mechanical Tumbler: 5in (13cm)
Gold mohair-over-metal; brown glass eyes, all jointed; key wound somersault; mint condition, rare. Circa 1950.
MARKS: No ID
PRICE: $500-up

Schuco Panda: 3½in (9cm)
Black and white mohair-over-metal; black bead eyes; excellent condition; all jointed; harder to find than mini bear. Circa 1950.
MARKS: No ID
PRICE: $125-up

Schuco "Soccer" Teddy Bear: 12in (31cm)
Brown mohair; black and white plastic eyes; plastic nose; felt tongue; soft stuffed; wears soccer clothes; excellent condition; reasonably easy to find.
MARKS: "Hegi" tag
PRICE: $75

Schuco Yes/no Rabbit: 5in (13cm)

Gold mohair-over-metal; brown glass eyes; red floss nose and mouth; felt-lined ears; all jointed; mint; hard to find. Circa 1950.
MARKS: No ID
PRICE: $250

Schuco Yes/no Penguin: 7½in (19cm)

Black and white mohair; red felt beak; tan felt feet; swivel head; soft and hard stuffed; scarves *appear* to be original; excellent condition; hard to find. Circa 1955.

MARKS: No ID

PRICE: $300-up

Schuco Yes/no Elephant: 5in (13cm)
Gray mohair-over-metal; felt ears and tusks; black and white glass eyes; mint; hard to find. Circa 1950.
MARKS: No ID
PRICE: $250-up

Schuco Yes/no Cat: 8in (20cm)

Gray mohair with black mohair behind velvet-lined ears; felt pads cardboard-lined feet; green glass eyes; excelsior stuffed; near mint; Very hard to find.

MARKS: "Tricky" tag

PRICE: $450

Schuco Yes/no Cat: 8in (20cm)

Same description except cotton under clothes; red and white cotton shirt; black felt pants; clothes not removable. It was common for Schuco to dispense with mohair (expensive even then) if clothes would cover. Good condition; rare. Circa 1950.

MARKS: No ID

PRICE: $250-up

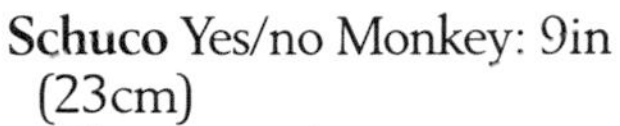

Schuco Yes/no Monkey: 9in (23cm)

Brown mohair; tan mohair inset face with white beard; tan mohair hands and feet; black glass eyes; felt ears; excelsior stuffed; all jointed; excellent condition; hard to find. Circa 1960.

MARKS: No ID

PRICE: $225

Schuco Yes/no Monkey: 4½in (12cm)

Brown mohair-over-metal; applied felt hands and feet; smoothly painted metal face; all jointed; mint; somewhat easy to find. Circa 1955.
MARKS: No ID
PRICE: $225.

Schuco Yes/no Monkey: 10in (25cm)

Brown mohair (faded in places); inset felt face; stitched to fingers felt hands and feet; felt ears; brown glass eyes; excelsior stuffed; all jointed; damage to felt face with straw showing; Monkeys are the easiest to find.
MARKS: "Tricky" tag
PRICE: $150

Schuco Yes/no Orangutan 15¾in (40cm)

Curly rust mohair; felt inset face, ears, and prehensile feet and paws; brown glass eyes; excelsior stuffed; all jointed; excellent condition; rare size. Circa 1950.

MARKS: No ID

PRICE: $500-up

Schuco "Noah's Ark" Squirrel: 3½in (9cm)
Gold shaded mohair; pipe cleaner limbs; yarn ears and tail; black bead eyes; holds yarn ball; tissue mint-in-box; somewhat rare.
MARKS: No ID
PRICE: $150

Schuco "Noah's Ark" Elephant: 2½in (6cm)
Gray mohair; black glass eyes; felt ears and tusks, red felt blanket; all jointed; mint; hard to find. Circa 1950.
MARKS: No ID
PRICE: $150

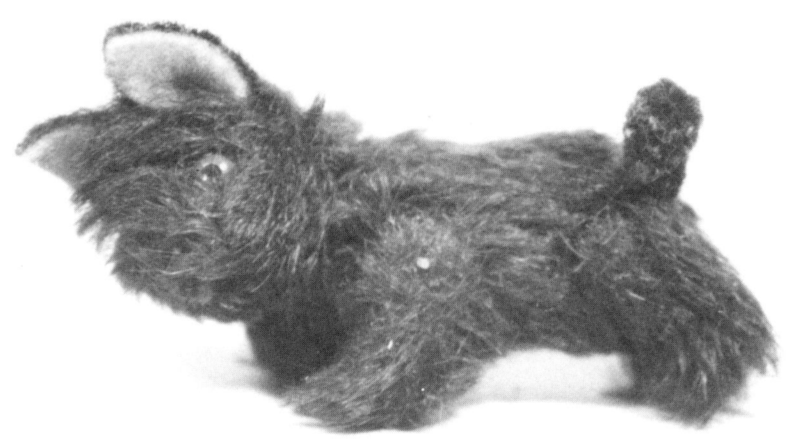

Schuco "Noah's Ark" Scotty: 2½in (6cm)
Black mohair; brown glass eyes; all jointed; felt tongue and inner ears; mint; fairly rare. Circa 1950.
MARKS: No ID
PRICE: $125

Schuco "Noah's Ark" Raccoon: 3½in (9cm)
Tan airbrushed mohair-over-metal; black bead eyes; felt-applied paws; all jointed; mint; hard to find. Circa 1950.
MARKS: No ID
PRICE: $150

Schuco "Noah's Ark" Pig: 3½in (9cm)

Pink mohair-over-metal; black bead eyes; felt ears and snout circle; all jointed; mint-in-box; pig is harder to find than others — more so with box. Circa 1950.

MARKS: No ID — except box

PRICE: $150

Schuco "Noah's Ark" Lion: 3in (8cm)
Gold mohair-over-metal; brown plush mane; black bead eyes; all jointed; mint-in-box; somewhat easy to find. Circa 1950.
PRICE: $150

Schuco "Mascott" Rabbit: 3½in (9cm)
Brown mohair head; pipe cleaner limbs; felt-lined ears and clothes; black and white eyes; excellent condition; somewhat hard to find. Circa 1967.
MARKS: No ID
PRICE: $105

Schuco "Mascot" Poodle: 2½in (6cm)
Black astrakhan plush-over-metal; brown glass eyes; felt tongue; all jointed; mint; hard to find. Circa 1950.
MARKS: No ID
PRICE: $125

Schuco "Mascot" Cat: 2½in (6cm)
Gray striped mohair-over-metal; black pipe cleaner tail; green glass eyes; felt-lined ears; all jointed; mint; hard to find. Circa 1950.
MARKS: No ID
PRICE: $150

Schuco "Mascott" Cats: 3½in (9cm)

White mohair girl; black mohair boy; pipe cleaner limbs; green glass eyes; felt clothes; mint-in-box; hard to find. Circa 1967.

PRICE: $75 each

Schuco Silly Cat: 7½in (19cm)

Gray mohair over bendable wire; velvet-lined black mohair ears; white, black and brown glass eyes; tongue; good condition; hard to find; no demand. Circa 1950.

MARKS: No ID

PRICE: $50

Schuco Bendable Wire Cat: 12in (31cm)
Black and white mohair; green celluloid eyes; yes/no by bendable wire; green cotton trousers; orange felt blouse; tissue mint; reasonably easy to find. Circa 1960.
MARKS: "Hegi" tag
PRICE: $50-up

Schuco Duck: 3½in (9cm)
Gold mohair; plastic eyes; felt beak, bendable wire body; dressed in felt sailor suit (clothes not removable); mint; reasonably easy to find. Circa 1968.
MARKS: No ID
PRICE: $85

Schuco Lion: 11in (28cm)
Natural colored plush; wire and straw stuffed; yellow and black plastic eyes; plastic nose; felt tongue; striped jersey shirt; felt boots; near mint; easy to find.
MARKS: "Hegi" tag
PRICE: $25

Schuco Dog: 11in (28cm)
Brown plush; wire and straw stuffed; brown plastic eyes; plastic nose; felt tongue; jersey shirt and shoes; near mint; easy to find.
MARKS: "Hegi" tag
PRICE: $25

Schuco *Lady:* 8in (20cm)
Tan, brown and white mohair; glass eyes with eyelashes; excelsior stuffed; plastic collar; mint; hard to find. Circa 1960.
MARKS: No ID
PRICE: $75

Schuco *Tramp:* 12in (31cm)
Brown and white mohair; black and white glass eyes; plastic nose; felt-lined open mouth; velvet lined ears; excelsior stuffed; squeaker; excellent condition; hard to find. Circa 1960.
MARKS: "Hegi" cloth tag in seam
PRICE: $125
Dogs are Walt Disney Production *Lady and the Tramp*.

Schuco Soccer Player: 15in (38cm)

Peach velour body; felt ears; plastic eyes; felt mouth with painted teeth; plush hair; swivel head; clothes removable except for socks; near mint; somewhat hard to find.

MARKS: "Hegi" tag

PRICE: $25-up

Carol Alabiso Collection.

Gebrüder Hermann

After the war the Hermann company relocated to Hirschaid, a small town near Bamberg in the western zone. They made quality Teddy Bears and animals and continue to do so today.

During the 20 years this book encompasses, they used a variety of tags. Materials ranged from a round paper to a triangular metallic. They often hung loose from a cord attached to the upper chest, a method easily torn off and no doubt responsible or its absence in most cases today.

A distinctive feature on their Teddy Bear faces is the sheared inset and rather squared muzzle. Three embroidered claws were used as well. Their "Zotty" bears can be confused with Steiff's, except if you remember that Steiff used a contrasting chest plate and Hermann did not. Not all of their bears had the inset snout but the majority of Teddy Bears from this era that appear on the market seem to do so.

Hermann Teddy Bear: 11in (28cm)
Caramel mohair; sheared inset snout; glass eyes; felt pads; all jointed; excelsior stuffed; excellent condition; somewhat easy to find. Circa 1955.
MARKS: No ID
PRICE: $135
Carol Alabiso Collection.

Hermann Teddy Bear: 16in (41cm)
Beige mohair; sheared snout; replaced pads; brown glass eyes; excelsior stuffed; all jointed; good condition; easy to find. Circa 1950.
MARKS: No ID
PRICE: $245

Hermann Teddy Bear: 14in (36cm)
Brown and tan frosted mohair; tan sheared snout and inside ears; felt pads; brown glass eyes; excelsior stuffed; all jointed; excellent condition; somewhat easy to find. Circa 1955.
MARKS: No ID
PRICE: $350

Hermann Teddy Bear: 15in (38cm)
Caramel mohair with sheared inset snout; felt pads; brown glass eyes; excelsior stuffed; all jointed; excellent condition; easy to find. Circa 1950.
MARKS: No ID
PRICE: $350

Brigitte Puckett Collection. Clothes not original.

Hermann Teddy Bear: 17in (43cm)
Light brown mohair; sheared snout; glass eyes; excelsior stuffed; all jointed; mint; somewhat easy to find. Circa 1950.
MARKS: No ID
PRICE: $350

Hermann Teddy Bear: 15¾in (40cm)
Caramel mohair; description same as above. Circa 1950.
MARKS: No ID
PRICE: $300

Ruth Baum Collection.

Hermann Teddy Bear: 14in (36cm)
Caramel mohair; tan sheared snout; brown glass eyes; replaced pads; all jointed; good condition; easy to find. Circa 1957.
MARKS: No ID
PRICE: $95

Barbara Chadwick Collection.

Hermann "Almost" Twin Teddy Bears: 10in (25cm) and 11in (28cm)

Tan mohair; inset sheared snout; brown glass eyes; felt pads (some replaced); excelsior stuffed; all jointed; good condition; somewhat easy to find. Circa 1950.

MARKS: No ID

PRICE: $245 each

Brigitte Puckett Collection.

Hermann Teddy Bear: 20in (51cm)

Tan mohair; short mohair inset snout; brown glass eyes; felt pads; excelsior stuffed; all jointed; excellent condition; easy to find. Circa 1955.

MARKS: No ID

PRICE: $250-up

Hermann Teddy Bear: 16in (41cm)

Tan mohair with inset shaved snout typical of Hermann; felt pads; brown glass eyes; excelsior stuffed; all jointed; wearing finely detailed gray felt lederhosen; mint; hard to find in clothes. Circa 1960.

MARKS: No ID

PRICE: $375-up

Hermann "Zotty" Teddy Bear: 14in (36cm)
Brown and tan frosted mohair; tan inset sheared snout; open felt mouth and pads; brown glass eyes; soft and hard stuffed; all jointed; squeaker; some mohair wear; somewhat easy to find. Circa 1965.
MARKS: No ID
PRICE: $150

Hermann "Zotty" Teddy Bear: 11in (28cm)
Beige and pale beige frosted mohair; sheared inset snout; open felt mouth and pads; brown glass eyes; soft and hard stuffed; all jointed; excellent condition; somewhat easy to find. Circa 1960.
MARKS: No ID
PRICE: $145
Brigitte Puckett Collection.

Hermann Teddy Bear: 9in (23cm)

Tan mohair with sheared snout and feet; open felt mouth and pads; brown glass eyes; excelsior stuffed; all jointed; nose ring and chain missing; good condition; hard to find. Circa 1960.

MARKS: No ID

PRICE: $200

Lorraine Oakley Collection.

Other German Companies

There were many makers of plush toys in Germany in the postwar era. Some, such as Grisly, continue their operation today. Grisly's identification mark is a round metal button firmly attached to the chest area. Airbrushed toes on sheared mohair pads are frequently used and can also be used as a reasonable guide.

Kersa used a metal plate on the sole and if that happened to dislodge, the marks from its application should be apparent. Their animals have a delightful charm but are not widely in demand; therefore, prices have not shown a sharp increase.

I think today most manufacturers are more aware of the value in marking their products in a more permanent way and finding value in accessing their archives. Unfortunately, this was not always true so many toys regretfully must remain as "manufacturer unknown."

Kersa Cat: 12in (31cm)
Black mohair; felt paw pads; green and black glass eyes; excelsior stuffed; all jointed; red felt hard-soled boots; excellent condition; adorable; hard to find but no demand. Circa 1948.
MARKS: Metal plate on left sole
"Kersa/made in/Germany"
PRICE: $100

Kersa Rabbit: 7in (18cm)
Light gold felt head, lower torso, legs and paws; black plastic eyes; orange felt sewed on blouse and shoes; excelsior stuffed; blue felt skirt; green felt apron; printed cotton scarf; painted circles for whisker starts; clothes not removable; excellent condition; charming and rare.
MARKS: Metal plate on left sole
"Kersa/made in/Germany"
PRICE: $125-up

Kersa Rabbit: 10in (25cm)
Brown wool plush head; peach felt body; black glass eyes; excelsior stuffed; cotton clothes; shirt paint spattered; grass filled basket on back; holding pallette; probably once held brush in right paw; near mint; rare.
MARKS: Metal plate on left sole
"Kersa/made in/Germany"
PRICE: $200-up

Clemens Teddy Bear: 8in (20cm)
Tan mohair; felt pads; brown glass eyes; all jointed; excelsior stuffed; excellent condition; reasonably easy to find.
MARKS: No ID
PRICE: $100

Clemens Teddy Bear: 24in (61cm)
Gold mohair; felt pads; brown glass eyes; excelsior stuffed; all jointed; mint; hard to find size. Circa 1955.
MARKS: No ID
PRICE: $500
Kay Skogland Collection.

Grisly Panda: 11in (28cm)
Black and white mohair; brown glass eyes; open felt mouth; airbrushed toes on foot pads (sheared mohair); soft and hard stuffed; good condition; somewhat easy to find.
MARKS: Button on chest
PRICE: $125

German Teddy Bear: 21in (53cm)
Beige mohair; sheared mohair pads and inset snout; glass eyes; excelsior head; soft body; all jointed; excellent condition, unusual appearance. Circa 1960.
MARKS: No ID; manufacturer unknown
PRICE: $95
Carol Alabiso Collection.

Grisly Rabbit: 7in (18cm)
Tan and rust mohair; brown glass eyes; excelsior stuffed; swivel head; mint; reasonably easy to find. Circa 1960.
MARKS: Metal tag on side; plastic tag in seam
PRICE: $60

German Teddy Bear: 19in (48cm)
Brown frosted gold mohair; velveteen pads; sheared snout; open felt mouth; brown glass eyes; excelsior stuffed; all jointed; growler; good condition; this type easy to find. Circa 1955.
MARKS: No ID; manufacturer unknown
PRICE: $285

German Teddy Bear: 13in (33cm)
Brown and white frosted mohair; felt pads; brown glass eyes; excelsior stuffed; all jointed; fur off snout; good condition; easy to find. Circa 1949.
MARKS: No ID; manufacturer unknown
PRICE: $225-up

Brigitte Puckett Collection.

German Twin Teddy Bears: 8½in (22cm)

Beige mohair; felt pads (hand replaced); excelsior stuffed; brown glass eyes; all jointed; some wear to mohair; somewhat hard to find a nearly matched pair. Circa 1948.

MARKS: No ID

PRICE: $140 each

Brigitte Puckett Collection.

German Teddy: 16in (41cm)

Black silky plush; felt pads; blue glass eyes; excelsior stuffed; all jointed; very long nose and hump; bib not original; supposedly 20 were found in a worker's house; mint; black in any bear is rare. Circa 1948.

MARKS: No ID

PRICE: $250

Kay Skogland Collection.

German Carnival Bear: 24in (61cm)

Pink and white frosted plush; tan wool snout; felt pads; all jointed; plastic eyes; excelsior stuffed; excellent condition; somewhat easy to find this style bear. Circa 1960.

MARKS: No ID

PRICE: $85

Brigitte Puckett Collection.

Unknown Teddy Bear: 16in (41cm)

Pale apricot mohair; glass stickpin eyes; linen pads; excelsior stuffed; all jointed; excellent condition. Circa 1950.

MARKS: No ID; origin unknown

PRICE: $225

German Panda: 16in (41cm)
Black alpaca and white mohair; black glass eyes; open felt-lined mouth; applied felt nose; excelsior stuffed; swivel head; mint; hard to find an exact duplicate.
MARKS: No ID; manufacturer unknown
PRICE: $250-up
Carol Alabiso Collection.

German Bear on Fours: 8in (20cm)
Brown mohair; brown glass eyes; open felt mouth; excelsior stuffed; swivel head; plastic collar; near mint; reasonably easy to find. Circa 1960.
MARKS: No ID
PRICE: $95
Barbara Chadwick Collection.

German Bear on Wheels: 12in (31cm)
Brown cotton plush; tan sheared plush nose and inner ears; soft and hard stuffed; brown glass eyes; metal frame and rubber tires; excellent condition. Circa 1960.
MARKS: No ID; manufacturer unknown
PRICE: $90
Susan Burdett Collection.

German Lion: 19in (48cm)
Gold mohair; brown and white frosted mane; black tail; brown glass eyes; airbrushed toes; slight hair loss; somewhat hard to find.
MARKS: U S Zone tag
PRICE: $125
Dennis Yusa Collection.

And Finally.....

The collecting of Teddy Bears and other soft toys crosses the boundaries of collecting in general, as perhaps in no other field. General antique lovers admire the charm of an older toy nestled among their candle molds (or whatever). I have sold Steiff tigers to a couple who had no interest in Steiff per se, but collected the striped beasts in every form. This is true of other animals as well.

How about collecting the items that are common? Do they deserve a place on our shelves? I would say yes. For a relatively modest investment, it is possible to amass a sizeable array of beautiful toys, in beautiful condition and most often with all labels. Then, too, we must remember that some day they will no longer be common.

We will make mistakes in buying or not buying. How easy it is to kick ourselves for passing by a treasure, or grinding our teeth in anguish for making a purchase that turned out to be a poor bargain at best. A few years ago I passed on a mohair studio size Irish setter. Now that my real life setter is in "doggie heaven," I wish twofold that I had that rememberance. Perhaps some day one will appear on my horizon. I hope your desires are fulfilled as well.

About the Author

Dee Hockenberry is author of the book *Bearers of Memories* and many articles about stuffed toys as well as being a Contributing Editor to *Teddy Bear and friends*® magazine. Also a bear maker, she sells her own bears through her Bears 'N Things business and, in addition, deals in collectible Steiff animals and Teddy Bears, with partner Lorraine Oakley.

Dee's photographer is her husband of 39 years, Tom Hockenberry. They have two children — a boy and a girl.

Notes

Notes

Notes